Table *for* One Chicago

The Solo Diner's Restaurant Guide

Michael Kaminer
and A LaBan

Contemporary Books

Chicago   New York   San Francisco   Lisbon   London   Madrid   Mexico City
Milan   New Delhi   San Juan   Seoul   Singapore   Sydney   Toronto

Library of Congress Cataloging-in-Publication Data

Kaminer Michael.
    Table for one, Chicago : the solo diner's restaurant guide /
Michael Kaminer, and A Laban.
        p.   cm. — (Table for one dining guide series)
    Includes index.
    ISBN 0-658-00698-3
    1. Restaurants—Illinois—Chicago—Guidebooks.
I. Laban, A   II. Title.   III. Series.

TX907.3.I32 C467   2001
647.95773'11—dc21   2001047550

Contemporary Books

*A Division of The **McGraw-Hill** Companies*

1 2 3 4 5 6 7 8 9 0   AGM/AGM   1 0 9 8 7 6 5 4 3 2

ISBN 0-658-00698-3

This book was set in Adobe Garamond
Printed and bound by Quebecor Martinsburg

Cover and series design by Rattray Design
Cover photograph copyright © Artville

McGraw-Hill books are available at special quantity discounts to use as
premiums and sales promotions, or for use in corporate training
programs. For more information, please write to the Director of Special
Sales, Professional Publishing, McGraw-Hill, Two Penn Plaza, New
York, NY 10121-2298. Or contact your local bookstore.

This book is printed on acid-free paper.

Contents

INTRODUCTION

THIS BOOK WAS borne of good and bad experiences dining solo in Chicago and around the world. I've been fawned over in Madrid by a maternal waitress who spoke no English, shoved into a suffocating communal table at a packed vegetarian dive in Paris, served with a smile in Bombay by the most solicitous waiters I've ever met, ignored at a cheap snack spot in Hong Kong buzzing with business-people on lunch break, and treated like royalty at a hotel dining room in St. Petersburg (Russia, not Florida).

In Chicago, dining solo may be an equally hit-or-miss proposition. In a city with an enormous number of single professionals and visitors, you'd think restaurants would welcome tables for one. But for every memorable meal I've experienced on my own, there's an infuriating experience I want to forget. With this book, I'm hoping to share some of those experiences to help make all of your solo meals a pleasure.

A little history: I've been dining out solo as long as I can remember, but really began appreciating the experience when I started my own business, back in 1992. After a twelve-hour day on the phone or talking to associates, the last thing I wanted after work was more talk. So I began blocking out dinner—to the extent I could—as private time.

It was, and still is, one of my most precious luxuries. It's pure pleasure to be able to visit a restaurant, choose my table, pace my meal, read, write, observe, savor, and quietly contemplate.

Chicagoans are lucky. Along with old standbys like neighborhood grills, ethnic eateries in storefronts, and coffeehouses, an abundance of more upscale places serve full menus at the counter or bar and otherwise welcome and accommodate solo diners. Sometimes you can tell by looking; sometimes (bad) experience is the only litmus test.

Another nice thing about dining out in Chicago is that many restaurants that don't have liquor licenses will allow you to bring your own. Corkage fees vary, but it always winds up being a better value than paying the typically horrendous restaurant markups. And, obviously, you will be drinking exactly what you want to be drinking. So grab your favorite half-bottle of wine and enjoy!

After all these years, I've developed some survival skills for the times when the meal's not so pleasant. As I imagine a lot of you have, I found complaining very difficult my first few times out alone. The last thing I wanted was to call more attention to myself. But after another lousy table, or another episode of apathetic service, or yet another waiter rushing me so a couple could take my place, I learned the value of raising my voice.

I hope I can help closet solo diners, who wish they could confidently request a table for one but secretly have nightmares about the scenario. For so many people, the primary emotion a table for one inspires is fear—fear of what others will think, fear that a restaurant won't treat them with respect, fear they won't be able to fill a long stretch of mealtime on their own. By proving that a solo meal can be a pleasure, I hope to help overcome that.

Luckily, there seems to be more awareness than ever of solo diners as a legitimate consumer force. Maybe it's the ever-increasing number of business travelers, maybe the spiraling number of single professionals. In any event, the net result seems to be better overall treatment by dining establishments.

"When I sit down to eat alone," Pamela Margoshes wrote recently in the *Washington Post*, "I am completely relaxed and happy in my own company. What could be wrong with that?"

What indeed?

I'm hoping to share that happiness with you in this book, as well as offer some caveats and tips gleaned from years of being both appreciated and abused by waitstaff:

Assert yourself.

If you're given what's obviously a lousy table, don't accept it. Complaining makes some solo diners uncomfortable, because no one is at your side to vouch for you. But nine times out of ten, my gripes have been validated (and apologized for) by a server or manager.

Sit near a window.

Nothing makes some solo diners more uncomfortable than being plopped at a two-top in the middle of a restaurant. A place by a window not only gives you choice seating on the periphery of the room, where you'll get the best view of the room, but also offers terrific people-watching opportunities if interest in your reading material wanes.

Pick a well-lighted spot.

Most solo diners I know love to read while they eat. You'll find it a lot more difficult if you have to squint at your newspaper through the gloom at a dimly lit corner table. If the lighting's abysmal, ask if it can be altered.

Avoid communal tables.

In theory, communal tables sound ideal. In reality, they usually re-create the dining ambience of an economy-class airplane flight.

Don't rush, and don't let them rush you.

Part of the pleasure of dining solo is the luxury of pacing yourself. Once, while dining at a San Francisco restaurant-of-the-moment, a waitress noted that I'd been sitting over my lunch for ninety minutes. I was about to get defensive when she told me how much she admired my ability to take time for myself and truly enjoy my meal.

Solo-friendly service is not necessarily proportional to price.

This is Chicago in the twenty-first century. Paying a lot for anything doesn't guarantee a good experience. The same holds true, sadly, for restaurants. As we discovered in the course of researching this book, many of the most expensive and exalted places treat solo diners the same way they'd treat a houseguest who'd overstayed his or her welcome. The point is, don't spend a lot of money on a meal just because you think it'll secure you special treatment. I've highlighted some of the better high-end places here to save you the trouble.

Make friends with servers and maitre d's, especially at places where you plan to return.

I can't count the number of times I've been given a table—for one—ahead of waiting hordes because I was friendly with a host, hostess, or server. You'll also find special requests and off-the-menu favors a lot easier to fulfill when waitstaff like you.

If a table's impossible, sit at the counter or bar.

Sometimes it is unreasonable to expect a table for one— strolling into a hot new restaurant at 8:00 on a Friday night, for example. But most respectable establishments will serve a full menu at the bar, which can offer a very pleasant alternative to a crowded room, if you don't mind smoke.

SOLO-DINING
SURVIVAL STRATEGIES

THEO IS ONE of the few people who actually wants to be in food service. He is an out-of-work sous-chef, as opposed to, say, another out-of-work actor or an out-of-work dot-com executive.

Like all of us, Theo has certain life occasions he likes to celebrate with a fancy meal. For birthdays and other special events, he calls up one or two of the city's top restaurants and makes a reservation for one.

Of course, not everyone has Theo's aplomb. For most of us, it takes a bit of luck and guesswork to outwit the system. One basic strategy is to arrive at an off hour—when the place is just opening, or after the main crush has left, but the kitchen is not yet closed.

A variation of Theo's idea works when you're from out of town. Most hotels have some sort of concierge service. Have the concierge make the reservation. There's a big difference between your calling up and saying, "I'm Joe

Shmoe. I'd like a table for one for 6:00 P.M." and the concierge calling up and saying, "Hi. I'm Tiffany. I'm the concierge at [your hotel]. We have a guest here who would like a reservation for tonight at 6:00." The restaurant may or may not take your reservation. The restaurant will likely take one from the hotel. The restaurant wants the hotel to recommend the place and to call again.

By the way, don't call up yourself and lie, either about being Tiffany or about the number of guests there will be. The host or hostess heard about the table for two, one of whom cancelled at the last minute, long before you thought it up.

As for tables, I don't mind being seated at a table in the bar. I also don't mind being seated near the kitchen or near a waiter's station. I look upon that as a way to attract attention that might not otherwise come my way. I know of one solo diner who would rather be at a table that faces a wall than "to face someone I'm not talking to."

Solo dining usually involves something to read or something to write. The newspaper is traditional, but a book or a magazine would certainly do as well. Whichever you pick, make sure that there's enough left to read to last you through your meal. I find a stack of two or three magazines works best.

Writing in restaurants is so popular that David Mamet used it as the title of a book. And just about any sort of writing will do. My friends ask where I find time to write a couple of hundred postcards whenever I go away. The answer is writing postcards at restaurants while I'm dining solo. My championship average is twenty cards per meal.

If fiction or correspondence isn't what you'd like to do, how about updating your planner? I can remember one waiter apologizing for interrupting my power lunch (for one) by bringing my order.

While playing with your Filofax is OK, working with a notebook is not, even if you remember to turn off all the bells and whistles. For some reason, pen and paper is intriguing while technology is intrusive. A handheld digital assistant is probably all right, but if your gizmo beeps, you are no longer asserting your right to your own space as a solo diner; you are now infringing upon the rights of others.

Also on the inadvisable list are beepers and cell phones. If you have to speak to someone during lunch, why didn't you ask that person to join you? And the table next to you won't be impressed with your importance. It will just be annoyed. Many people are convinced that whoever is calling them or interrupting them is much more important than what they're doing. Don't let yourself be interrupted at the table and don't interrupt others.

In addition to the suggestions I've already made, here are a few basic concepts to help you be a successful solo diner wherever you may go.

Know thyself.

It's all very well and good for me to tell you to assert yourself. I live in Chicago. I'm case-hardened. You have to know the stress levels at which you are still able to function and work within them. If you're shy, asking for a table for one at an off hour at a local restaurant is quite an accomplishment. Work your way up before you tackle single bookings at four-star restaurants.

Think strategically.

Think before you feed. As much as I hate to admit it, dining solo sometimes involves a trade-off. Don't try restaurants during their rush hours. Outwit them. Figure out when they'd love to see you. Look for off hours, like 6:00 to 7:00 P.M. or 9:00 to 10:00 P.M. Clues they want your business might be early bird or pretheater specials. Prix fixe is also a subtle hint that a place is looking.

Take a chance.

Try a brand-new place no one has reviewed yet—or a cuisine you've never heard of. Often, these restaurants are trying to build business and will see you as a potential "word-of-mouth" influencer to get everyone you know to try them out as well.

Travel light.

Don't bring a lot of preconceived notions about how solo diners, or even you as a solo diner should be treated or will be treated. Be open to adventure. That empty chair across from you at the table next to the kitchen door might well be where the chef takes his or her break.

Finally, if you're reading this book, you're probably familiar with the ever-changing Chicago restaurant scene. Today's hot ticket is tomorrow's "for rent" sign. All of the listings in this book were verified at press time. You'll want to call and confirm details. You can also check for updates at the official Table for One site, table-for-one.com. Happy solo dining!

About the Reviews

Price Key:

$ = less than $20
$$ = $20 to $40
$$$ = $40 to $60
$$$$ = more than $60

Prices are per person (of course), including dessert and one glass of wine.

Rating Icons:

𝄞 = Service		5 = superior	
♟ = Lighting		4 = very good	
𝄢 = Food		3 = good	
♟ = Selection of wines by the glass		2 = barely adequate	
♙ = Comfort/placement/number of small tables suitable for solo diners		1 = abysmal	

Note: the absence of a rating for wine selections means the establishment does not serve wine. They may, however, allow you to bring your own and charge a corkage fee. They may also serve other alcoholic beverages, including beer and mixed drinks.

The Loop, South Loop, West Loop, Greektown

The head that sits on the city's big shoulders is, arguably, found in the Loop. Chicago's center of business, the Loop is the home of the Merc and the city's two other exchanges, numerous businesses, and the hustle and bustle of shopping on State Street, all of which are served by the El lines that find their nexus downtown.

The Loop and its surrounding appendages that have increasingly stretched south and west offer some interesting options for a diner on his or her own. Once a ghost town after offices closed, the Loop proper now offers a number of choices to serve theater crowds, making it easier if you want to enjoy dinner and a show on your own.

While the South Loop has become increasingly residential, restaurants haven't kept up in the neighborhood nearly at the pace that they have in the West Loop, where eating establishments sprouted among the meatpacking operations long before the West Loop's lofts came to dot the landscape along Washington and Randolph. Solo diner beware, however; the West Loop has become so trendy, it's

7

become increasingly difficult to find a quiet table for one where you can hear yourself think or where you won't feel pressure to vacate in favor of a trendy table for two.

Greektown remains an overrated tourist attraction. But students at the nearby University of Illinois at Chicago campus—as well as the draw of the United Center directly west—keep the neighborhood hopping and continue to create some off-the-beaten-track options that may appeal more to a solo diner than Halsted's cavernous Mediterranean eateries serving mediocre food serenaded by shouts of "Opa!" If you explore off Halsted, you'll lose your view of the downtown skyline, but you may just find some hidden gems.

Bar Louie
123 North Halsted
312-207-0500

47 West Polk
312-347-0000
See page 19.

The Berghoff
17 West Adams
312-427-3170
$

This bustling beer hall is accustomed to serving individual tourists and Loop diners ducking out of their offices. A Chicago institution, The Berghoff opened as a corner saloon in 1898 and has been serving up schnitzel, knockwurst, and the ever-popular sauerbraten with spaetzle at its current location since 1913. Diners should stick with the German favorites and not take a chance with the menu's more diverse (read: inevitably bland-to-bad), mainstream options. Same with the beverage menu; stick with a stein of Berghoff beer instead of a glass of wine. P.S. If you don't feel like sitting down, you can always grab a sandwich at the adjoining Berghoff Cafe, a stand-up bar that's particularly good for a quick lunch.

Blackbird
619 West Randolph
312-715-0708
$ $ $

Blackbird was a West Loop pioneer and remains a hot spot. Its European-influenced, contemporary American food is ever changing. Exquisite service is exacting—but the seating arrangements are excruciating. With its impossibly tight lineup of tables squeezed along its east wall, Blackbird is the kind of place where everyone not only knows your name, but also knows practically everything else about you; so you'll be thankful you're alone. While polite diners may work hard to ignore each other, it's not unusual to get stuck with a nosy neighbor who will assure you that your dinner selection is right on. As if you need to be told; it's hard to miss at Blackbird. A seasonal menu incorporates fresh produce to create entrees like wood-grilled California sturgeon with Yukon gold potatoes and celery root hash; braised oxtail au jus and pickled red onions; and osso buco with artichokes, red-wine roasted shallots, bone-marrow gnocchi, and gremolata. Blackbird's sidewalk patio offers some relief from the restaurant's close interior quarters; take advantage of it during nice weather before you're penned up for the winter again. Solo diners can also eat at the bar, a good bet when Blackbird is particularly crowded. Lots of interesting boutique wines, although more by the bottle than the glass.

Buddy Guy's Legends
754 South Wabash
312-427-0333
$

Although Buddy Guy's is a must-visit on many a tourist's itinerary, many locals have never been there. That's a shame, because the club offers a full evening of modestly priced live blues nightly, along with a tempting menu of Southern specialties. Bigger than many of the city's blues clubs, Buddy Guy's offers plenty of room for its tables, a good view of performances, and friendly waiters serving shrimp Creole, jambalaya, and barbecued ribs, among other comfort food typical of the Mississippi Delta. Local acts usually perform during the week, with nationally recognized names on the weekend. Jam sessions are Mondays. Forget the wine; this is a beer and mixed drink place. P.S. The volume level here means you probably won't be reading a book during dinner.

Catch Thirty-Five
35 West Wacker
312-346-3500
$ $ $

This cavernous seafood restaurant in the Leo Burnett building attracts a convivial mix of locals, tourists, and conventioneers. Even on a busy Saturday night, the packed room doesn't get loud or obnoxious, which makes it a good bet for solo diners looking for a relaxed Loop alternative. In fact, a row of small booths in an elevated back section of the restaurant makes an ideal perch for a table for one. Fish makes the menu here, and it's perfectly cooked; most of the selections involve healthy-looking cuts of tuna, salmon, snapper, or swordfish. Timid sides, like green beans and carrots, don't match the main attractions. The organic baby lettuce salad with goat cheese makes a fine starter, and the delicate pan-seared sea bass with Szechwan soy glaze is practically translucent. What really stands out is Catch Thirty-Five's wine list; it offers an astonishing selection of wines by the glass, including varietals you rarely see outside a full bottle. Service is smooth and friendly, though food runners seem to need a vacation. P.S. Lighting is subdued but good enough to read by.

Garden Restaurant (Art Institute of Chicago)

111 South Michigan

312-443-3543

$ $ 🍴 🍴

🥢 🥢   🍸

🍷 🍷 🍷   🍴 🍴 🍴 🍴 🍴

Has wandering around the Art Institute made you hungry? If the weather's warm, head for the Garden Restaurant. Because it's ensconced in the middle of the museum, finding this outdoor restaurant is something of a treasure hunt. But once you locate the staircase next to the Old Stock Exchange room off the Columbus Drive entrance, you'll enter another world. Shaded by towering trees, serenaded by a burbling fountain decorated with mermen, the atmosphere here encourages you to linger and daydream. While the house wine leaves something to be desired, the menu overall is light and summery, with soups, fruit plates, salads, a burger, pizzas du jour, even sushi. Tuesday evenings, the Garden stays open late for an evening of jazz, but arrive early to get a good table among those who exercise squatter's rights. P.S. Cold-weather options at the Art Institute include the Restaurant on the Park and the Court Cafeteria, an inexpensive but less charming option that shares the same kitchen as the Garden Restaurant.

Grace

623 West Randolph

312-928-9200

$ $ $

You've got to feel pretty confident about your kitchen when you set up shop on a relatively barren strip in the West Loop, a location distinguished only by being next door to Blackbird. Grace, however, holds its own in comparisons with its much-talked-about neighbor. With an emphasis on "new American" cooking, Grace features game—dishes like wild blackberry–stuffed venison loin, wood-grilled saddle of rabbit in a juniper berry–port wine prune sauce, and grilled, herb-crusted wild boar tenderloin served with cinnamon-chili white cheddar polenta and nectarine compote. The less adventurous can try dishes like moist and flavorful pan-roasted chicken breast with wildflower honey glaze and sage-andouille cornbread stuffing, or the black Angus rib-eye steak with white truffle potato puree and zinfandel-peppercorn sauce. In contrast to Blackbird, Grace's loft-like interior has been softened with some judicious drapings, and tables are better spaced, so you won't have to sit in the lap of the stranger next to you. Overall, the dining atmosphere is far calmer and less frantic than Blackbird's, so if you're seeking a quieter table for one, you may want to choose Grace over its neighbor. Reservations recommended, even for one.

Jaks Tap
901 West Jackson
312-666-1700
$

It shouldn't take long for fans of the Village Tap on Roscoe to recognize the menu at Jaks Tap. Owned by the proprietors of the Roscoe Village establishment, Jaks serves the same extensive selection of well-prepared bar food in a neighborhood pub that's friendly but sleek, as befits the increasingly sleek West Loop area. Solo diners can also get a seat and linger, an impossible feat these days at the ever-popular Village Tap, except during off-hours. Soups, salads, quesadillas, burritos, and burgers—all served with a choice of fries or rice and beans—populate the menu, and everything tastes a lot better than typical short-order bar grill food. The veggie burrito, a weighty cylinder of Mexican delight, is the Solo Diner's favorite. Along with a "margarita of the day," Jaks boasts "the largest draught beer selection in Chicago," a selection that appears to be weighted toward ales and lagers. Service isn't all that attentive, but if you're downtown and want a convenient place to grab a beer and burger, watch a game, or just hang, you'll do well here.

onesixtyblue
160 North Loomis
312-850-0303
$ $ $

An elegant power restaurant a hop, skip, and jump away from the United Center on the edge of the West Randolph restaurant strip, onesixtyblue might be a bit overwrought for solo dining, but excellent contemporary American creations make it worthwhile for a night out. The menu changes seasonally and is structured to encourage a three-course meal, with options like the signature peekytoe crab "sandwich" as a starter; entree of rare duck breast with shredded duck leg over butternut squash risotto with dried cherries; and a cheese plate or caramelized banana napoleon with white chocolate ice cream for dessert. Lots of fish and seafood options round out the menu. Excellent service will ignore the fact you're on your own, and nicely spaced tables give you plenty of privacy. You can eat dinner and absorb the see-and-be-seen scene in the sleek lounge with leather banquettes and a zinc-topped bar. Good wine list. Reservations recommended.

Rhapsody
65 East Adams
312-786-9911
$ $ $

As part of Symphony Center, Rhapsody offers a perfect option for the solo diner in search of a complete evening. A team led by chef de cuisine Jon Novak and pastry chef Erika Masuda—whose bios read like a who's who of Chicago dining—this team remembers that food needs to taste as good as it looks. Signature starters include a sautéed duck foie gras served with cauliflower flan, candied ginger, and a sweet onion sauce rich enough for dessert. Entrees range from striped bass with asparagus and mimosa sauce to the roasted rack of lamb with Moroccan couscous, baby carrots, and fennel confit. Save room for the chocolate symphony for dessert. Service is as impeccable as the food, even for tables for one. Savor it all in Rhapsody's white and natural-wood dining room with well-spaced tables looking out through floor-to-ceiling windows on a small urban garden.

Taza
39 South Wabash
312-425-9988
$ 🍴 🍴 🍴

It's surprising that Taza hasn't spread across the city like Starbucks. After all, this eatery serves some of the freshest, tastiest, best-priced grilled chicken in town, and it offers a quick bite to grab on your own at lunch or dinner in a bright, clean dining room that's several notches above any other Loop fast food. Chickens at Taza—which you're told over and over means "fresh" by the restaurant's assorted personnel—are raised on Amish farms and shipped at twenty-three days old, rather than the usual forty-six. The tender young birds are then marinated in fresh citrus juices, grilled, and turned into any number of global chicken-based dishes. Sandwiches range from the Jamaican jerk chicken pita to the avocado and sprout-enhanced California club to the sun-dried tomato, pesto, and mozzarella-topped Milano to the surprise combo of the day. Salads are ecumenically ethnic and include a Chinese chicken breast and a Greek salad. Insatiable solo diners can opt for the straight-up whole, charcoal-grilled twenty-ounce chicken. Taking freshness to the limit, cooked chickens are held only ten minutes; after which they're donated to the Chicago Food Depository. Tastes great, costs less, and supports a good cause. No alcohol.

Wishbone
1001 West Washington
312-850-BONE (2663)

$

Solo diners at Wishbone's two cavernous restaurants aren't treated any better or worse by the harried waitstaff than are couples or much larger parties, but you will be encouraged to outflank the crowds if you spot an open counter seat. Both locations (see page 67 for Lakeview address), decorated with the signature Wishbone chicken paintings, are packed morning and evening with devotees of the popular brand of Southern comfort, including corn cakes, jambalaya omelets, hoppin' John, and yardbirds, a quarter charbroiled chicken served with two sides. If you're going for brunch, get there before 10:00 A.M. or be prepared to wait. Lots of screaming kids, so avoid like the plague if you're child-averse.

MICHIGAN AVENUE,
GOLD COAST,
RIVER NORTH

MICHIGAN AVENUE—the buzz of One Mag Mile—dulls to a funky melody among the galleries of River North and then a hum in the quiet, tony neighborhood of the Gold Coast. Although solo diners have plenty of options for grabbing a bite after hours of work or shopping in these neighborhoods, prices tend to be high and higher unless you look hard.

Michigan Avenue tends to appeal to the day crowd, with many of its evening restaurant options being targeted at those with a (hotel) room with a view. Lunch options abound, but dinner can be either stuffy or more of a production than you're looking for, unless you choose one of the bargain-priced alternatives found among the high-rises.

The artists of River North tend to sleep and eat late, but the neighborhood offers some of the more interesting eating options in the city, although many of them may be too much of a see-and-be-seen scene for a party of one to feel comfortable. Meanwhile, adjacent to the Rush Street nastiness that solo diners should steer well clear of are the quiet, elitist blocks of the Gold Coast and a couple of quiet eateries tucked away serving the neighbors and those who know where to go.

Akai Hana
848 North State
312-787-4881
$ $

Just west of Michigan Avenue, casual Akai Hana offers a welcome rest stop after a grueling day of shopping. Lots of small tables and a good-sized sushi bar make it easy for solo diners to get a seat and hold on to it until the feet recover. You may have to track down a server when the place gets crowded, though. Akai Hana also provides surprisingly cheap (and fresh) sushi to a neighborhood accustomed to paying for location. Monday through Friday, the "sushi regular"—six pieces and a roll, soup, and ice cream—is ten dollars. Vegetarian options abound, including a succulent sweet potato tempura roll. P.S. A recent revamp of the menu has added more entree options and has left lunch a better deal than dinner, which is not as much of a bargain deal as it used to be.

Albert's Cafe
52 West Elm
312-751-0666
$ $

An oasis of calm just five minutes from the hustle and bustle of Oak Street and Michigan Avenue, Albert's is a small patisserie and white-tablecloth European bistro in a cozy space whose main feature is an impressive pastry case. Solo diners will feel at home; it's common to see neighborhood locals sitting alone catching a quiet meal here with the paper or a book. A popular place for a coffee-and-dessert break after a day of frenetic shopping, the cafe also offers homemade soups, salads, cheese plates, and heartier fare for dinner. The Solo Diner has enjoyed rosettes of beef tenderloin, tricolor tortellini with cheeses and herbs, and fricassee of chicken, as well as richer dishes like eggs Benedict and Belgian waffles with fresh fruit and Grand Marnier sauce.

Bar Louie

226 West Chicago

312-337-3313

$

The original Bar Louie and still the best, the River North location is decorated with the colorful tiles and bright murals that have become the signature look at the other locations. All of these joints have become so popular that the only negative for solo diners—and everyone else—is getting a seat at the bar or one of the small tables. Strategic dining is imperative. Regardless, Bar Louie is a good place to relax and enjoy Mediterranean food a cut well above typical pub grub. With an abundant menu heavy on Italian selections, Bar Louie offers pastas, pizzas, meal-sized salads, antipasti, and panini. In clement weather, the River

North location treats its patrons to sidewalk tables with a well-positioned view of a truly picturesque stretch of Chicago Avenue, where you'll be serenaded by the low hum of the Ravenswood El.

Bice Grill
158 East Ontario
312-664-1474
$

Bice Grill is the low-budget next-door offspring of one of Michigan Avenue's longtime see-and-be-seen spots and a great place to grab lunch or carry out an early dinner on your own. Self described as a "high-end cafeteria," Bice Grill offers an ever-changing selection of salads, soups, panini caldi (warm sandwiches), pizzas, and pastas. Pasta is the real deal, with a "small" serving from the daily selection of three pastas—you can mix and match—running only $4.50. Other solo-friendly options are good-sized salads (grilled chicken optional) and hot sandwiches served with a cup of red sauce for dipping. P.S. Sorry, but dibs on that fancy, tablecloth-clad spot outside the front door belong to the fancy, tablecloth diners at Bice next door.

Big Bowl
159½ West Erie
312-787-8297

6 East Cedar
312-640-8888

60 East Ohio
312-951-1888/312-951-9888

Another creation from Lettuce Entertain You, the Big Bowl restaurants offer reasonably priced, fast and fresh, Americanized versions of Asian dishes in a stylishly designed faux-Asian environment. The numerous small tables are relatively close together, but many of them will be occupied by solo diners grabbing a quick bite with a paper or book. They move 'em in and out here, so you won't be able to linger long, and service can be a bit harried, but it's almost always friendly. Food is dependably tasty, prepared without MSG, and served in a smoke-free dining room. The steamed or fried dumplings with various fillings and kung pao chicken are always a good bet, as is the fresh stir-fry, in nearly thirty different combinations. Mixed drinks, like the gin-gin cooler (homemade ginger ale laced with gin) or mai tai, are typically a better bet than the wines.

Brasserie Jo

59 West Hubbard
312-595-0800

Looking for a pleasant solo dinner that evokes memories of your favorite Parisian bistro? Try Brasserie Jo. A casual French restaurant with a turn-of-the-century Parisian feel, it is owned by chef Jean Joho of four-star Everest fame. The restaurant's Alsatian menu showcases the artistry of one of Chicago's top chefs in a straightforward and affordable setting, with options like onion tarts, choucroute, coq au vin, and fillet of skate. Brass rails and a zinc bar create a festive feel. Alsatian wines are featured, as are French and Belgian beers and "Hopla," brewed by Baderbrau exclusively for Brasserie Jo. Bistros and brasseries have traditionally been havens for solo diners and Brasserie Jo is no exception. Just stay away on weekends when the place gets packed and noisy with suburbanites and tourists.

Le Colonial
937 North Rush
312-255-0088
$ $ $

In this elegant pre-Colonial Vietnamese environment, you can relax in peaceful rooms that are furnished with wicker chairs and potted ferns under ceiling fans that gently churn the air. While the pricey menu is all Vietnamese, with specialties like *ca chien* Saigon (crisp-seared whole red snapper), *ca hap* (steamed fillet of sea bass with cellophane noodles, mushrooms, scallions, and ginger), and *mi xao don chay* (crispy noodles with tofu and stir-fried mixed vegetables), French influences permeate the wine list, which has selections from Burgundy, Bordeaux, the Loire valley, Alsace, and Champagne, many of which are available by the glass. In spite of its elegant atmosphere, Le Colonial has an unfortunate reputation for spotty service that's out of sync with its expensive setting. Some feel you're better off—food, price, and service-wise—farther north at Pasteur (page 80). Solo diners should also avoid the sidewalk seating in the summer, unless you really want to be scrutinized by the crowds of strolling shoppers. A good option if you've been out shopping on Michigan Avenue; you can order from the full menu at the bar if the restaurant's busy.

Cru Cafe & Wine Bar

888 North Wabash

312-337-4078

$ $

A great place to linger by yourself after a long day of shopping, or just for people watching on a nice day from the sidewalk seating here. Once the well-known Third Coast coffeehouse, Cru has been spiffed from a crumbling coffee shop to an elegant wine bar, and service has vastly improved, although it retains more attitude than necessary. The menu remains essentially light, sometimes to a fault; a couple of sad-looking grapes accompany stingy flights of regional cheeses. In contrast, the pasta salad is bountiful and bursting with the flavors of the Mediterranean, a rare thing for usually bland noodle salads. Other "hearty" fare includes the Cru Club, a lobster club sandwich, and charcuterie plates. The astonishing wine list is a boon for solo diners, who can order by the glass from more than four hundred wines in the cellar. Beware; leather club seating in the back alcove is for cigar and pipe smokers.

foodlife

Water Tower Place

312-335-3663

$

Michigan Avenue shoppers and businesspeople alike flock to foodlife, a kinder, gentler, and definitely tastier food court offering a wide variety of snazzy food stations. Food is tasty, and presentation is slick, but at the end of the day, foodlife is still a food court in a shopping mall, so you'll see plenty of solo diners here. The emphasis is on healthful eating; Mother Earth Grains, the Roadside Hamburger Stand, and the Miracle Juice Bar share the space with the inevitable coffee stand, Sacred Grounds Espresso Bar, as well as pasta, Mexican, Asian, salads, and an impressive dessert counter. Self-service.

Ghirardelli Chocolate Shop & Soda Fountain

830 North Michigan

312-337-9330

$

For those who need a sugar buzz to keep moving, Ghirardelli, just off the Michigan Avenue's densest shopping area, has some sweet options. You'll see plenty of solo shoppers making a pit stop to indulge in guilty pleasures on their own. Serving only ice cream and chocolate, not so much as a sandwich here, decadence comes in good-sized helpings. "World famous" sundaes should be more than enough; don't even think about trying the mammoth Earthquake Sundae, created for four, on your own. Designed to look like an old soda shop, Ghirardelli's has a long bar, a checkered floor, and ceiling fans. A gift shop sells chocolate to go.

Heaven on Seven

600 North Michigan
312-280-7774

111 North Wabash, 7th Floor
312-263-6443

$ $ 🍴 🍴

👥 👥 👥   🍷 🍷

🍽 🍽 🍽   🎭 🎭 🎭

Woo, doggy! Looking for a nonstop Mardi Gras party packed with tourists and local faithful? Check out the daily Cajun carnival at Heaven on Seven. Being just one block off Michigan Avenue in the same building as a multiscreen movie theater makes Heaven on Seven a good option of an evening's entertainment for any solo diner. The loud, party atmosphere will make it difficult to relax and read anything here, but the labels on some twenty different bottles of hot sauce that decorate every table are quirky and interesting. They're enough to keep a solo diner entertained. However, the food, although abundant, is overrated.

Hi Ricky Asian Noodle Shop & Satay Bar

941 West Randolph
312-491-9100
See page 93.

India Garden

247 East Ontario, 2nd Floor
312-280-4934/4910
See page 77.

Isaac Hayes Restaurant
739 North Clark
312-266-2400

$ ¶ ¶ ¶

🕴 🕴 🕴   ⅄

🍶 🍶   �a� �a� �a�

A new partnership between Isaac Hayes and an out-of-town chain founded by Humboldt Park native Dave Anderson, this restaurant brings Anderson's reverence for the holy trinity of "Smoke, Meat, and Sauce" back to his hometown. Portions at Isaac Hayes's are as big as the live music blasting out nightly from the main stage. You'd think such a raucous atmosphere would discourage solo diners. But because Isaac Hayes is not far from Michigan Avenue, single business travelers and tourists are common here for an evening of barbecue and live nightly entertainment. You might as well be alone, since it's too loud to have a conversation with anyone here. Focus on the food instead; meat comes slathered with Dave's "butt rockin'" special sauce, a tangy topping with kick. Brave souls can try the All-American Feast—a full slab of ribs, a whole chicken, half a pound of beef brisket or chopped pork, coleslaw, fries, and some of the tastiest roadhouse beans around. It's so big it's served on a garbage-can lid. Oh, and try to save some room for the "World Famous" bread pudding, a slab drowned in vanilla ice cream, whipped cream, and maple syrup. As you might've guessed, beer and booze are better options than wine here.

Joy of Ireland
Chicago Place
700 North Michigan, Level 3
312-664-7290

$

This quaint Irish shop in Chicago Place now serves an enjoyable high tea in a cozy tearoom that's complete with Irish newspapers and magazines to help you while away the time while your tea steeps. The half-dozen tables, perfect for solo diners, afford an impressive view of Michigan Avenue and offer a perfect rest stop after hours of shopping. Teas include Irish brands like Taylors of Harrogate, Fortnum & Mason, Barry's, Brewley's, and Yorkshire Gold. Irresistible baked goods include homemade scones, petit fours, coffee cake, fruit tortes, cookies, sweet bread, and brown bread (sold by the slice or the loaf). Joy of Ireland also serves a light lunch with soups, salads, a cheese plate, a smoked salmon plate, and plates of finger sandwiches like smoked salmon and cucumber–cream cheese, as well as an assortment of cheeses.

Oak Street Beachstro

Oak Street Beach at Oak and Michigan

312-915-4100

$ $

It's all about location, location, location; rarely has a restaurant gotten diners so close to the water. Solo beachcombers in hordes wander up-sand to enjoy a bite and a nonalcoholic strawberry daiquiri with a view at Oak Street Beachstro. And the Beachstro is a full-fledged restaurant—no trumped-up short-order grill here. Though you'll find burgers and sandwiches, the restaurant's aspirations run more toward herb-crusted beef tenderloin and sautéed salmon filet. Pastas; rock shrimp with broccoli and tomato tossed in garlic oil; and grilled chicken with spinach, sun-dried tomatoes, and mushrooms in a butter-Parmesan sauce are good-sized and tasty. Chase it all down with a piña colada frozen smoothie. Desserts include Key lime pie and the "world's best strawberry sundae." P.S. No shirt or shoes required, though you may want to don both in colder months.

Puck's at the MCA
Museum of Contemporary Art
220 East Chicago
312-397-4034
$ $

For those of us who prefer exploring museums on our own, it's nice to have a more sophisticated refueling stop than McDonald's. And, there are plenty of solo art and maybe just culinary fans at Puck's, because you don't need to be a member of the MCA to enjoy the restaurant and its menu of Mediterranean and Asian-influenced cuisine. Puck's features Wolfgang Puck's well-known pizzas, as well as a number of more filling entrees, including meat loaf wrapped in pancetta and served with roasted garlic-potato puree, a mountain of grilled onions, and port wine sauce; a flavorsome roasted rosemary chicken with mashed potatoes and red wine sauce; and grilled salmon paillard with braised autumn vegetable provençal for lunch and dinner on Tuesdays. Service can be excruciatingly slow, but no pokier for solo diners than for anyone else, and, in a dining room bright with a flood of natural light, you'll be able to comfortably read all about the current exhibitions while you wait it out for your food. P.S. Most of the sandwiches and salads, including the classic Spago Chinois chicken salad, are available at the carryout counter, where you can get your meal a lot quicker and sit down on the opposite side of the room from the restaurant. Enjoy patio dining in the summer under arty umbrellas looking out over the lake. Stake out one of those prime spots for an afternoon.

Reza's
432 West Ontario
312-664-4500
See page 80.

The Signature Room on the Ninety-Fifth
John Hancock Building
875 North Michigan
312-787-9596

$ $

🍴 🍴

♟ ♟ ♟   ♟ ♟ ♟

♟ ♟ ♟   🏛 🏛 🏛 🏛

This room with a view being inside a major tourist destination, the waitstaff are used to solo diners dropping in to see the skyline, which can't be beat. The $13.95 pig-out lunch buffet makes this one of the Mag Mile's hidden gems. All the other à la carte items on the lunch menu—sandwiches, salads, pastas—are also a pretty good deal but fairly pedestrian, so stick with the buffet. Dinner is significantly more expensive, and the Solo Diner doesn't find it any better tasting. P.S. Lunch is served Monday through Saturday, 11:00 A.M. to 2:00 P.M.

Toast

228 West Chicago

312-944-7023

$ 〃 〃 〃 〃

🜲 🜲 🜲   ⊻

♟ ♟ ♟ ♟ ♟   ⋔ ⋔

A kitschy, funky brunch place that plays heavily on the theme of its name, Toast puts some decadence into the early morning meal, with French toast, crepes, and at least three different kinds of eggs Benedict, including "crabby" eggs and a veggie version for non–meat eaters. Other healthful options include tofu veggie crepes, and, as long as you're not vegan, numerous omelet options. A lunch menu is available, but no one orders from it. You'll notice lots of solo diners reading papers and books here, but the waiting crowds will apply some pressure on lingerers if the waitstaff don't. Tables are a tight squeeze, so you may feel more relaxed at one of the many counter seats if there's a crowd. Only open for breakfast and lunch. P.S. Early-day spirits only—mimosas, Bloody Marys, screwdrivers, and Sierra Nevada beer. No wine.

The Wolf & Kettle Coffee Shop

101 East Pearson

312-915-8595

$ 〃 〃

🜲

♟ ♟ ♟ ♟   ⋔ ⋔ ⋔ ⋔

You might expect a rest spot affiliated with the church to be peaceful, and the Wolf & Kettle delivers, offering a quiet refuge from the hustle and bustle of North Michigan Avenue. A coffeehouse owned by the Jesuits of Loyola University, the Wolf & Kettle offers coffeehouse fare, including pastries, salads, sandwiches, and even assorted maki rolls, all of which can be washed down with Big Gulp–sized cups of coffee. The coffeehouse's heavy wood furniture looks like it was stolen from Loyola's library, and its combination of booths, tables, and couches offers a fair amount of lounging space where students and weary shoppers can put their feet up to read or just veg. Solo diners can also while away some time perusing the captions on the old photographs hanging on the walls, which include pictures like *The Flying Sophomore*, a black and white of student skater Lars Lundgcot taken in 1925. You'll also see a memorial certificate commemorating the fiftieth anniversary of Loyola's Law School and its Papal blessing by Pope Pius XII. Reputed to stay open late during Loyola final exams weeks, but not open Saturday or Sunday. Cash only.

Zoom Kitchen
923 North Rush
312-440-3500
$

Zoom Kitchen's got the ingredients for a perfect meal when you're out for a bite on your own: comfort food with a healthy twist served fast in a sparkling clean, stainless-steel environment. If the cafeteria-like line begins to back up in front of the salads, move down to sandwiches, fresh carvings, and hot and cold side dishes. Standouts include low-fat chicken sausage and portabella mushroom sandwiches (opt for their suggested condiment combos, or select your own from choices like chipotle mayonnaise, caramelized onions, and avocado spread), as well as hunks of fresh meat loaf and turkey loaf. Breads at the Bucktown location come from Red Hen Bakery right around the corner. The place fills up with locals at mealtimes, adding to that homey feel. Finish off with a reassuring slice of pie. All-you-can-eat eight-dollar brunch served Sundays. More Zooms seem to open every day, so watch for new ones. No alcohol.

LINCOLN PARK

FABLED LINCOLN PARK, long a desired address for yuppies and wanna-bes, is a disappointment for solo diners. Over-crowded, overpriced, and overrated, unless you're willing to be a little creative, you'll have to work awfully hard to find a comfortable table for one.

The problem with Lincoln Park is that, not only is there practically an absence of anything remotely ethnic, but there simply isn't a lot to eat that falls between four-star restaurants (like Charlie Trotter's) and the sports bars that dot the landscape and serve both DePaul students and for-mer DePaul students and those from nearly every other Midwestern school you can think of. That being said, you don't have to resign yourself to wings or nachos and a stool in a corner.

Solo diners looking for a meal in Lincoln Park simply have to commit to the hunt: first for a parking space, if you are unwise enough to drive, and then for a cozy table at a neighborhood place that's not wall-to-wall with Bears fans—eyes glued to multiple screens—and/or drunken students looking for a companion for the evening. It can be done, particularly as you drift west from the lakeshore, in the part of the neighborhood between Halsted and Clybourn. Sure, there are some good options on the lake, but you're going to have to look hard.

Ann Sather
2665 North Clark
773-327-9522 (carryout only)
See page 44.

Bar Louie
1800 North Lincoln
312-337-9800
See page 19.

John's Place
1200 West Webster
773-525-6670
$

John's is a solid, warm, welcoming neighborhood place; it's as comfortable for large groups who wait for tables at brunch as it is for the solo diner with a newspaper who may happen in any time during the day. The menu is mostly traditional American fare spiked with ethnic dishes, including spiced catfish wraps mingled with soba noodles, turkey cobb salads, and sandwiches with sweet potato fries. Get up early if you don't want to face a long wait for John's crabby eggs, crab cakes with poached eggs and homemade salsa; chocolate banana pancakes; or smoked salmon scramble. P.S. John's is known for being kid-friendly, so beware if you were looking for peace and quiet.

Marco! Ristorante Italiano

2630 North Clybourn

773-348-2106/2450

$ $

No "red sauce" trattoria here. Chef Marco Conti, who previously owned La Risotteria Nord, infuses his cooking with the richness of Northern Italy. His well-edited menu features four different risottos, including the classic risotto asparagus and saffron, as well as several veal dishes. The Solo Diner is especially partial to osso buco alla *cremolata*, veal shank served in a creamy pancetta and porcini mushroom sauce that was a standout back at La Risotteria Nord. Fish and seafood dishes here are fresh and generous, and the pasta of the day is usually something special and surprising, like ravioli stuffed with pheasant on a pool of truffle butter. Conti also prides himself on his selection of unusual wines from small vineyards in Italy, and he will be happy to spend time with you explaining them. Solo diners can hide away at one of the tiny tables in the tiny balcony and will be treated like one of the family on the main floor. Otherwise, ask to sit as far as possible from the bar bordering the south side of the room—unless you enjoy smoke or want to feel like you've just developed the habit.

North Pond Cafe

2610 North Cannon Drive

773-477-5845

$ $ $ 🍴 🍴 🍴 🍴 🍴

🍶 🍶 🍶 🍶 🍶   🍸 🍸 🍸 🍸

🔔 🔔   🛎 🛎 🛎 🛎 🛎

Tucked into the leafy dell of Lincoln Park between Stockton and Cannon Drives at Diversey, this cozy, Prairie-style restaurant—once a warming house for ice skaters—is an urban oasis with service as gracious to solo diners as it is to groups. It specializes in a contemporary American cuisine that often incorporates fresh local produce and complements its menu with an extensive, mostly American wine list. North Pond makes a relaxing escape lunch (seasonal), dinner, or Sunday brunch, and, given its bucolic setting, is one of the few upscale restaurants in the city where you actually feel like you should be lingering over a classic novel. At dinner, start with avocado and peekytoe crab salad, and then move on to pan-roasted, boneless pheasant with fresh fava bean ragout, morel mushrooms, and fresh spinach. Brunchers enjoy a three-course prix fixe menu that might include diet-busting options like hazelnut pancakes and orange-vanilla French toast. In warm-weather months, you can enjoy the covered terrace, which overlooks placid North Pond and offers a sweeping view of near North Michigan Avenue towering over the greenery and sleepy ducks. Lunchtime provides built-in entertainment from the playground next door (though the two are separated by a row of tall bushes). North Pond isn't visible from any of the roadways, though, so call ahead for specific directions and parking recommendations.

Pasta Palazzo
1966 North Halsted
773-248-1400

Most fans of Italian can't say enough about this brightly decorated, tile-walled neighborhood eatery, where "short order Italian grill" has been raised to a fine art. Solo diners can grab a seat at the counter and watch the grilling action or can pull up a chair at one of the high, broad tables that give you a sense of dining family style, even if you're alone. Although prepared simply and priced to be penne-wise (everything on the menu is less than ten dollars), Pasta Palazzo's dishes are as zesty as more highbrow trattorias; favorite options include handmade gnocchi and tortellini along with pasta standards and risottos. Cash only.

Penny's Noodle Shop

950 West Diversey

773-281-8448

See page 59.

The Red Lion

2446 North Lincoln

773-348-2695

Named for Edward III's heraldic device, the Red Lion serves a traditional English menu that has probably been popular since Edward's day in the mid-fourteenth century. True to its pub heritage, the Red Lion helps solo diners feel comfortable stopping in for a pint and a bite—you won't feel alone by the time it's time to go home, because this is the rare kind of place that cultivates a community. If you've cultivated an appetite, try starting your meal with Welsh rarebit or a serving of beans on toast. Then move on to bangers and mash (sausages and potatoes) or a mixed grill (Canadian bacon, American/"streaky" bacon, baked beans, mashed potatoes, and grilled tomatoes). If you're only hungry for a lighter bite, you can try a pasty or a pie—that would be a Cornish pasty, shepherd's pie, or steak and kidney pie. Finish it off with a serving of English trifle. Enjoy the nice patio in warm weather. Wine is available, but you should stick to the good selection of imported beers and mixed drinks.

The Red Rooster Wine Bar & Cafe

2100 North Halsted
773-929-7660
$

Rarely crowded, the Red Rooster will allow you to take a seat by yourself at one of its twelve tables and linger. Located in the heart of Lincoln Park, it's a quiet oasis of French provincial cuisine designed to let you tuck yourself away for a peaceful evening. The sister restaurant to fancier next-door neighbor Cafe Bernard, this rustic, cabin-like bistro displays its menu on a chalkboard on the wall. Selections are refreshingly affordable, and the emphasis is on hearty, traditional French bistro cuisine. Options include mustard chicken, beef stroganoff, and duck à l'orange, along with classics-with-a-twist like smoked chicken sausage over angel hair pasta, spinach fettuccine with sea scallops, and grilled salmon in cabernet sauvignon sauce. Pâté is a good start, and crème brûlée is a good end.

Shallots
2324 North Clark
773-755-5205
$ $ $

The thought of traditional Jewish dinner might bring bland brisket to mind. But there's nothing boring about the dishes at Shallots, probably the only gourmet kosher restaurant in Chicago, and one that treats single diners with as much care as groups. Shallots forgoes seafood, pork products, creams, and butter sauces, and still manages to crank out impressive dishes, many of whose Mediterranean flavors reflect the traditional cooking of "Oriental" Sephardic Jews. Lamb *tagine*, for example, combines chunks of tender lamb with dried apricots, figs, and dates in a spicy sauce, served on a bed of couscous; with the entire dish being delivered to your table in a traditional Moroccan tagine pot. Chilean sea bass is prepared with Moroccan spices and poached in a spicy tomato fennel broth with lentils and figs. Meat and game have more of an American twang; venison medallions are served with roasted chestnuts, sweet potatoes, winter squashes, and a dried cranberry–red wine sauce. Only a limited grill menu is served on Saturday nights. All this kosher purity comes at a relative steep price, but it's one worth paying. If you're alone in your dietary concerns or you simply want a unique meal, you'll feel comfortable at a table for one at Shallots.

LAKEVIEW

IF THE CITY's not careful, Lakeview will soon be indistinguishable from Lincoln Park—an enclave for overweening yuppies and transient post-collegiate renters looking for their next frat party. But, thanks to Lakeview's solid neighborhoods, the area may never homogenize to the whitebread, overpriced eating typically found in Lincoln Park.

Neighborhoods like Boys Town, the rapidly gentrifying Roscoe Village, up-and-coming St. Ben's, and the Southport Corridor continue to create interesting eating options, typically in small settings that will make the solo diner feel at home. Even Wrigleyville offers some gems among the raucous sports bars that crowd the landscape outside of Wrigley Field.

Halsted between Addison and Belmont, where the boys are, offers ongoing support to casual, creative cooking, while Roscoe between Lincoln and Western continues to sprout eateries where you can enjoy a well-priced, tasty meal and a good novel. Southport between Irving Park and Diversey offers numerous table-for-one options, many of which are in close proximity of the Music Box Theatre, well-known for its foreign and independent films, giving diners (solo and otherwise) a dinner and movie option for a complete evening.

For those on a real budget, Lakeview continues to support numerous ethnic storefronts, lots of Latin and Asian options, including the small Indian enclave near the Belmont el stop.

Plenty of options for solo diners of all stripes, all of whom should take advantage of convenient public transportation—don't even think about trying to find a place to park.

A La Turka
3134 North Lincoln
773-935-6447
$ $

A La Turka's modest storefront belies a lush, fabulous interior, with a ceiling draped like a tent and terra-cotta-daubed walls. You'll find both Turkish-style seating on cushions at low tables and standard Western options, all nicely spaced to allow you a virtually private show when the belly dancer does her rounds. (If this sort of entertainment makes you uncomfortable, call to see when it takes place. It's not every night.) The menu is extensive and loaded with tasty, tangy Turkish/Middle Eastern options for both the carnivore and the vegetarian. The best plan for solo diners to taste with abundance is to order a hot or cold appetizer combination and, if you've got big eyes, an entree. You may end up feeling stuffed liked a vegetable yourself, however. Wash it all down with sips of Turkish coffee or tea, served in tiny glasses so hot they should come with a temperature warning. Lighting is a bit dim, but sufficient to grab a pillow, lean back, and enjoy a couple chapters of *A Thousand and One Nights*.

Abbey Pub

3420 West Grace
773-463-5808
$

Opened in 1973, the Abbey Pub is one of the "true Irish" places in a city that prides itself in wearing its green heart on its sleeve. And, like a real Irish pub—a home away from home—diners are as welcome here solo as they are in groups of ten. It's not, however, the place for a quiet evening with the paper; be ready to join the crowd, enjoy live music, and take in what seems to be constant broadcasts of football (the kind the rest of the world plays). No-frills but tasty Irish pub food includes Irish stew and shepherd's pie. The traditional Irish breakfast, served 9:00 A.M. to 2:00 P.M. on weekends, makes it worth rising early to beat the crowds. A Spartan atmosphere with a big screen TV for big events, including World Cup Soccer, Gaelic football and hurling, and Chicago's own local heroes. Open stage nights on Tuesdays for the bard in you, while Sundays feature Irish jam sessions and Mondays host the weekly Barn Dance. Entertainment schedule is at abbeypub.com.

Ann Sather

929 West Belmont

773-348-2378

3416 North Southport

773-404-4475 (carryout only)

$ 🍴 🍴 🍴

🛎 🛎 🛎   🍸 🍸

🪑 🪑 🪑 🪑   🚪 🚪 🚪

Ann Sather has been serving its renowned cinnamon buns, Swedish breakfasts, weighty lunches, and dinners loaded with Swedish comfort food since 1945. The environment's always been so casual and comfortable you can not only show up alone, but you can also show up solo in your pajamas. In the morning don't miss the thin Swedish pancakes with the lingonberry preserves; order a side of Swedish potato sausage for extra oomph. Later in the day, indulge in Swedish meatballs, dumplings, duck breast glazed with lingonberries, potato and veal sausage, and (generally over-cooked) vegetables. Cinnamon buns to go are $7.50 a dozen. An extensive bar includes hot, spiced Swedish glögg. Skip the inevitable wait at Belmont by heading north to the Andersonville branch (see page 71). Regardless, during the morning, you and your server may feel a bit pressed by the crowds. Only the original Belmont location is open late (past 3:30 P.M. weekdays, 5:30 P.M. weekends).

Anna Maria's Pasteria

3953 North Broadway

773-929-6363

$ 🍴 🍴 🍴 🍴 🍴

🛎 🛎 🛎 🛎   🍸 🍸

🪑 🪑 🪑   🚪 🚪 🚪 🚪

With its success over the years, Anna Maria's has expanded from a former Spartan storefront into three fancy rooms with warm golden walls, wine-colored drapes, and tablecloths—comforts few would expect to find at Irving Park and Broadway. But at heart, Anna Maria's is still a neighborhood joint where even solo diners are treated like family to unbeatable penne puttanesca, rotola aurora (vegetarian rolled pasta with ricotta cheese and spinach in a creamy tomato sauce), and a truly magnificent veal marsala even better than your mama can make. Save room for dessert.

Bar Louie
3545 North Clark
773-296-2500
See page 19.

Beat Kitchen
2100 West Belmont
773-281-4444

$ 🍴 🍴 🍴

Like most eateries that are inherently neighborhood bars, Beat Kitchen is a casual and comfortable stop for solo diners. Its nightly music option makes it a good place for an entire evening on your own. Having re-emerged from a fire that very nearly destroyed it, Beat Kitchen continues to feature a menu as eclectic and intriguing as its live music. Some forty items fall under the headings of salads, soups, sandwiches, and pizzas, including a Beat salad (pear, bacon, blue cheese, egg, red pepper, avocado, red onion, and toasted pine nuts tossed with honey Dijon dressing) and the

Beatburger. Gourmet pizzas range from prosciutto-Asiago to sun-dried tomato pesto with Japanese eggplant and caramelized onions to a breakfast pie featuring eggs, mushrooms, green peppers, red onions, bacon, and jalapeño jack cheese. A huge smoked salmon plate piled high with thinly sliced Norwegian salmon, diced onion, tomato, avocado, egg, and capers is a pleasant surprise, even for a place that has moved well beyond pub grub.

Blue Stem

1935 West Irving Park
773-665-1340
$ $

An elegant but comfortable neighborhood eatery, Blue Stem often gets overlooked on a lackluster stretch of Irving Park sandwiched between up-and-coming St. Ben's and the outer limits of Lakeview. That's too bad, because the small tables in a cozy space make Blue Stem a good option for solo diners. Named for Illinois's official prairie grass, the restaurant is owned by a husband-and-wife cooking team that focuses on a seasonal, health-conscious regional American menu that changes frequently. Starters can include a delicious chunky tomato-basil soup or barbecued duck tenderloin skewers with mango and mint salsa. The New York strip steak—the litmus test of any "American" specialist—is tender and comes with rich sides like shiitake mushroom sauce and roasted garlic mashed potatoes; there's also a daily fish special and daily vegetarian dish, like white bean and mushroom stew served with polenta, walnut pesto, and goat cheese enchiladas. Desserts like strawberry-rhubarb crisp with vanilla ice cream or crème brûlée with ever-changing flavors are a perfect way to finish things off.

Brett's

2011 West Roscoe

773-248-0999

$ $

This casual neighborhood restaurant is an urban oasis, warmly accommodating nearly any party size, including solo diners. Patrons come clad in everything from ties to T-shirts to dine in one of the most attractive and airy rooms in the city. Besides its setting, Brett's secret of success is a seasonal focus on dishes that feature Asian, Latin, Caribbean, and good old American flavors in combinations that fuse rather than fight. Unlike global fusion combinations so overdone around town, the matches here work; entrees like red snapper with *mojo de ajo* (garlic sauce) and white bean puree, jerk pork chop with macaroni and cheese, and grilled loin lamb chops with olive sauce and maple sweet potatoes are all harmonious and delicious. Although the seasonal menu is updated frequently, crowd-pleasers like grilled flank steak with sesame ginger sauce and sautéed spinach are usually available. While a mélange of flavors may characterize starters and entrees, desserts shoot straight. There's no monkeying around with creations like chocolate cigars and fruit sushi; instead, there are jumbo slices of classic chocolate cake, deep-dish cobblers, and creative sorbets. The weekend brunch, with warm homemade breads and jams and seasonal specials like pumpkin waffles, is one of the best in the city and not to be missed, although brunch is when Brett's gets really crowded, so you might feel some pressure to eat faster. P.S. Bargain hunters, take note: Nightly fifteen-dollar prix fixe dinner before 6:30 P.M.

Cafe 28
1800 West Irving Park
773-528-2883
$ $

Cafe 28 serves traditional Cuban and Mexican dishes with flair in two cozy (some might say cramped) relatively noisy rooms decorated in warm colors, with twinkling white lights. Standing-room-only crowds line up for this family-owned restaurant's interpretation of Latin dishes; solo ingles are treated warmly, but be prepared to wait like everyone else. The menu includes *ropa vieja* (literal translation, "old clothes"), beef slowly simmered in garlic tomato sauce until it falls apart, and Cuban roast pork, succulent slices topped with caramelized onions and garlic. Cafe 28's *estilo nuevo*, or new-style, dishes include options like citrus-marinated salmon wrapped around julienned seasonal vegetables and baked, almond-crusted halibut baked in a saffron cream, and beef tenderloin with saffron risotto. Most entrees come with hefty sides of white rice and black beans—usually enough for a solo diner to both feast on and take home. Weekend brunch.

Cafe Le Loup
3348 North Sheffield
773-248-1830

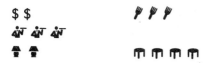

An established, cozy Lakeview eatery with plenty of small tables and friendly service, Le Loup has long offered some of the best deals in town on cassoulet, *poulet Breton*, *boeuf bourguignonne*, and pork loin *forestiere*, all of which can be enjoyed year-round at a table for one in the restaurant's covered garden. Many of Le Loup's dishes have a Mediterranean bent and include couscous or *merguez*, the spicy North African lamb sausages, so you can sit outside in the depths of Chicago winter and imagine yourself being caressed by warm breezes blowing over the beaches of Morocco or Tunisia. If you prefer to eat indoors, you can enjoy a vegetarian or ratatouille crepe under the watchful eyes of the many namesake wolves (*le loup* means "wolf" en francais) that decorate the walls while you finish off your meal with a chocolate mousse or crepes flambé. The garden's busy in the summer, but the pace is slower in colder months, when you can linger as long as you'd like. BYOB.

Chicago Diner

3411 North Halsted
773-935-6696

Arguably the best-known vegetarian restaurant in the city, Lakeview's Chicago Diner remains a magnet for the healthy, and its comfortable booths and plenty of counter seats make the Chicago Diner a good place for solo diners to hang out and readjust their metabolisms. As the name implies, the place is diner-friendly and the focus is on comfort food, but delivered with a veggie or vegan twist; you'll find lots of seitan, a wheat-based meat substitute. The lengthy list of entrees includes baked grain burgers, Reubens made with grilled tempeh, lentil loaves, tofu loaves, and macrobiotic plates. Latin accents in some of the options add some spice.

La Creperie
2845 North Clark
773-528-9050
$

For nearly thirty years, La Creperie, has been a good place to park yourself with a book or paper for a casual lunch or dinner. It serves nicely priced dinner crepes and plump dessert crepes. Sheets of buckwheat are folded around broccoli and cheese, spinach creme, ratatouille, chicken curry and rice, or other fillings. Dessert crepes range from creme de marrons to Grand Marnier and Suzette à la Germain. Three-course meals priced under twenty dollars include choice of soup or salad, buckwheat entree crepes with choice of filling, and a choice from more than a dozen dessert crepes. Non-crepe entree items include orange roughy or steak frites. If you're on your own, you might want to head to the back and avoid the smoky front room with a dark bar that's frequently serenaded by accordion music. Service can be very French, meaning rude and slow. And be forewarned: it's kind of a date place. Cider, the traditional beverage to serve with crepes, is available, as are plenty of wines by the glass, carafe, or bottle. Or, sip a cup of strong French coffee while you linger.

Cy's Steak & Chop House

4138 North Lincoln

773-4040-5800

$ $

If you're looking to get fattened up, Chicago has no shortage of steakhouses that can do the job. But Cy's, a neighborhood steakhouse that offers downtown tastes at neighborhood prices and in portions that aren't too obnoxious, is a pleasant alternative for those on their own. The restaurant's two rooms feature floor-to-ceiling windows that open on nice days, ceiling fans that whirl lazily under a copper ceiling, and nicely spaced booths for plenty of privacy. Meals begin with a basket of warm bread and sides of baked garlic and scoops of soft, sweet butter—a perfect and simple starter for Cy's wide selection of prime and dry-aged meats. Make sure you save some bread—or better yet, ask for another loaf—to soak up the optional red wine–garlic or bourbon-mushroom butter you should order with your steak.

Deleece

4004 North Southport

773-325-1710

deleece.com

$ $

Once an oddity on the northern edge of Lakeview—an eatery that bridges the gap between neighborhood restaurant and more upscale dining place—Deleece is now a mainstay in an ever more affluent community. It's also a perfect setting for solo diners, with smallish tables that feel just right for singles. Housed in a renovated grocery store with exposed brick walls, burgundy velvet drapes, and black accents, Deleece looks more Wicker Park than Wrigleyville, and the menu is much more consistent with what's usually served at the intersection of Damen and North than at the numerous sports bars in the area. Entrees typify the global fusion trend that has swept the city, with an emphasis on Italian and Asian flavors. The coconut-curry marinated chicken breast served with sesame-mint couscous and peanut sauce is an unexpectedly tasty combination of Southeast Asia with the Mediterranean, as is the Asian-inspired bouillabaisse with giant prawns, scallops, mussels, cod, and bass in a tomato-lemongrass–star anise broth. Sunday brunch starts at 10:00 A.M. P.S. Solo diners may feel pressured to eat quickly and leave when Deleece gets busy, especially during the packed brunch on the weekends, so dine strategically.

The Duke of Perth

2913 North Clark

773-477-1741

$

The Duke of Perth, like classic pubs, accommodates parties of all sizes, and those dining or drinking solo may find they soon have a group of new friends at this typically crowded and sometimes noisy local favorite. This place serves all-you-can-eat, beer batter–dipped cod accompanied by peas and chips from lunch until midnight on Wednesdays and Fridays, which alone makes it worth the trip. In addition, the pub offers other Highland specialties, including Scotch eggs—a breaded sausage wrapped around a boiled egg with sweet chutney—steak and kidney potpie, shepherd's pie, and sides of stovies. Thankfully, there's no haggis. Good old American burgers are dedicated to Scottish heroes with accompanying tributes, including the William Wallace cheeseburger for the braveheart who was "hanged, drawn, and quartered with his head then impaled on London Bridge." Think about that as you squirt ketchup and mustard on the meat. There's not much in the way of wine so try a dram from one of the Midwest's most extensive collections of single-malt scotch—seventy-five in all—or choose from the nice selection of beers from the UK and Scotland. P.S. There's a patio with picnic tables in clement weather and often live Celtic music on Saturday nights.

The Golden Apple

2971 North Lincoln

773-528-1413

$

Night owls must thank their stars daily when they see this restaurant's radiant neon apple sign here. Open 24/7, the Golden Apple holds its own with any other diner in the city—any day, any hour. Some half-dozen pages of well-priced breakfast, lunch, dinner, and dessert options should satisfy your cravings, no matter what they are or at what time you're having them. A good-sized counter is an option when the place is crowded, as booths are tough to come by for solo diners. The menu has a Mexican twist, like the breakfast burrito, a huge roll of beans, cheese, guacamole, tomatoes, lettuce, and meat accompanied by spicy rice, an excellent way to start your day or end your evening. P.S. There's pleasant sidewalk dining under an awning here in nice weather.

Hi Ricky Asian Noodle Shop & Satay Bar
3737 North Southport
773-388-0000
See page 93.

Jim's Grill
1429 West Irving Park
773-525-4050
$

A tiny, nondescript diner, you can count the number of tables at Jim's on one hand (with fingers left over). Stools at the two small counters can also be hard to come by, although congenial strangers will typically allow you to squeeze in next to them and will probably even share some conversation with you. Chat with the regulars while you choose among a variety of standard, short-order grill breakfast options or from the more exotic Korean selections on the menu. Regulars' favorites include the vegetarian pancakes; mounds of vegetables stir-fried in a rice-based batter served with a tangy sauce; *bi bim bop*; a rice bowl served with a fried egg and stir-fried vegetables (chicken, beef, or pork optional); or one of the daily Korean specials—hot, spicy noodles one day, vegetarian maki rolls the next. Wash it all down with an assortment of traditional Korean teas, including barley and ginger. No alcohol.

Joy's Noodles and Rice

3257 North Broadway

773-327-8330

$

Its solo-friendliness alone would be enough to recommend Joy's, an unassuming Lakeview Thai spot. But the big surprise here is the food—incredibly fresh and flavorful Asian favorites that belie their below-average prices. Tom yum soup is clean and piercing, with the lemongrass and citrus flavors upfront and strong. Noodle dishes are generous and spicy; curry dishes are vibrant; and vegetables are invariably fresh and cooked right. You'll see a number of contented solo diners here constantly; an accommodating crew of roving servers keeps them, and everyone else, very happy. Excellent lighting; comfortable back patio in warm weather.

JT Collins

3358 North Paulina

773-327-7467

$

If you're looking for a quintessential neighborhood watering hole where you can be at home away from home and where, even alone, you're never really alone, look no further than JT's. A former Rexall drugstore, this wedge-shaped bar has two walls of floor-to-ceiling windows that can be opened on balmy days to sidewalk seating. Food is a cut above typical bar fare; the burger of choice here is the spicy chicken burger, while the cheeseburger is stuffed with Gorgonzola. Flatbread with chicken sausage, shredded Parmesan, spinach, gorgonzola, tomatoes, and a small side salad is more than enough for a meal. For those looking for something heartier, there's a roasted, marinated chicken; pastas; and assorted kabobs. Come on your own and plan on spending a couple hours—everyone else does too.

Karyn's Fresh Corner

3351 North Lincoln
773-296-6990
$

Karyn Calabrese, Chicago's local raw foodie and a major supplier of natural sunlight-grown wheat grass, also runs what she calls a "living foods garden cafe." That means patio tables, turf, a raw food buffet, an oxygen bar, and a culinary regimen that attracts hardy, proud, and often solo diners (Karyn says her own husband tends to eat to a different cooked and sometimes carnivorous drummer.) Food is raw and vegan, and entrees range from mock tuna or turkey to a delicious almond pâté. Counter service sandwiches include a veggie burger with lemon-tahini sauce and a seed-cheese *nori* roll made from fermented sunflower seeds and pumpkinseeds. Karyn offers periodic detox workshops for those who have fallen off the wagon; the group support is great, but given the side effects, you'll definitely want to pursue on your own. Additional one-on-one counseling and a number of other services are available from

Karyn at her Inner Beauty Center farther south on Lincoln.
No alcohol. No meat. No preservatives. Self-serve.

Kitsch'n on Roscoe
2005 West Roscoe
773-248-7372
$

Solo diners actually enjoy an advantage at Kitsch'n on
Roscoe. We can sit at the counter, a refuge when it gets
really crazy here and the best way to avoid the long line.
With its Crayola-bright Formica floors, linoleum tables,
and multihued vinyl chairs, Kitsch'n pays homage to the
1970s, but the menu is definitely weighted in our era. Breakfast includes creative selections like Tang martinis, Giant
Pecan Waffle, and Green Eggs & Ham with spinach pesto.
Lunch offers the best fried-chicken club sandwich around,
served with root veggie chips, fries, or mashed potatoes, as
well as daily TV Dinner specials, which are also served at
dinner Fridays and Saturdays. The waitstaff is some of the
best in town, whether they're hunting down pieces of Mr.
Potato Head for shrieking kids, gently organizing a long,
still-half-asleep table line characterized by a bad case of
bed head, or making friendly small talk with a solo diner.
Beer and mixed drinks only.

Lakeview Restaurant & Pancake House
3243 North Ashland
773-525-5685
$

One size generously fits all, whether you're a party of one or ten, at the Lakeview Restaurant & Pancake House. An old-fashioned mix of coffee shop and diner, the Lakeview has a friendly staff accessorized in black aprons with leopard-patterned packets, plump pink vinyl booths, full-swivel counter seats, and a warm welcome for solo diners in the booths (when it's quiet) and at the counter (always, especially if you don't mind smoking). The giant menu overwhelms with a half-dozen pages of options. It's all here, from hearty breakfasts, skirt steaks, butt steaks, rib-eyes, and pork chops fried up with eggs, to heavy-duty dinners served with soup or salad, potatoes, rolls, coffee, and dessert. Drop your dining pretensions and dig into fried chicken, a hot breaded veal cutlet patty, or the pork tenderloin. For something a little lighter, opt for a tomato stuffed with a choice of chicken salad, tuna, or egg salad (side of cottage cheese, hard-boiled egg, and fruit included) or the diet plate, with a choice of chicken breast or hamburger. Opens early, closes late.

Melrose Grille & Breakfast House

3233 North Broadway
773-327-2060
$ 🍴🍴🍴🍴
🎩🎩🎩🎩🎩
👤👤👤👤👤 🛏🛏🛏🛏🛏

There are diners and there are diners, and then there's Melrose—home of football-sized omelets, motherly waitresses, and this town's most hopping men's scene outside the Boys Town bars. Solo diners of all persuasions feel welcome here; no matter how busy it gets, the harried hosts always seem to find a table for one. At peak hours—which can come late here, when bars close, and late weekend mornings—the counter's not a bad option, with a close-up view of the kitchen and good eavesdropping on servers. The coffee-shop lighting is perfect for reading, and Melrose even keeps an overflowing shelf of newspapers at the entrance. Stick with the basics—breakfast is served around the clock, since the place is open 24/7—and you can't go wrong.

Outpost

3438 North Clark
773-244-1166
$ $

The Outpost offers white tablecloths and downtown taste in a casual neighborhood atmosphere. It's a pleasant combination that stands out on a street dominated by Wrigleyville's rowdy sports bars. Its seasonal menu blends eclectic, global flavors in busy-sounding dishes like seared ostrich with pistachio-crusted goat cheese and roasted duck breast in orange reduction with duck confit and a compote of wild rice, tart cherries, caramelized almonds, and mushrooms. Outpost's pride is a magnificent, gleaming wood bar that stocks a huge variety of wines from around the world, many of which are served by the glass in ever-changing, special tasting programs. Many of the waitstaff have been here since it opened, and they are as friendly to regulars—many of whom dine here once a week—as they are to first-time strangers. Brunch is as good a bet as dinner. A caveat: On weekends, it's difficult for this place to accommodate singles who want to get a table and linger.

Penny's Noodle Shop

3400 North Sheffield
773-281-8222

1542 North Damen
773-394-0100
$ 🍴 🍴 🍴
👤 👤 👤 👤
🍽 🍽 🍽 🍽 🍽   🛏 🛏 🛏

All of Penny's locations are typically packed, so be prepared to wait if you can't nab a counter stool. They are also cozy and clean, with cooking designed to appeal to scores of less adventuresome eaters; the restaurant and staff are both fresh-scrubbed, service is always with a smile, and solo diners are as welcome as larger groups. Entrees have a Thai twist and include variations of noodle soups, noodles in a bowl, stir-fried noodles, and rice plates. All are six dollars and under. P.S. The Sheffield location offers sidewalk seating, and the Damen location offers the most room. BYOB.

Piazza Bella

2116 West Roscoe
773-477-7330
$ $ 🍴 🍴 🍴 🍴
👤 👤 👤 👤 👤   🍸 🍸 🍸 🍸
🍽 🍽   🛏

Given the many tables stuffed into its modest space, Piazza Bella is actually more comfortable for a table for one than for any more than that. This cozy little neighborhood trattoria produces downtown tastes at neighborhood prices; its menu of Italian specialties—presented in Italian with English subtitles—range from old-fashioned gnocchi della mamma and lasagna della nonna ("homemade lasagna like grandma used to make") to the more flamboyant ravioli di carni, four coaster-sized ravioli with mushrooms, asparagus, and cherry tomatoes. There's also a constantly changing cav-

alcade of specials. Dinners, served with a salad, are generous; the Solo Diner's favorites include the veal dishes and
two tangy chicken options, namely pollo al limone, a
chicken breast sautéed with white wine, capers, lemon
sauce, and croutons; and pollo alle erbe, a chicken breast
pounded and grilled with fresh herbs and served on a bed
of grilled vegetables and balsamic vinegar. Salmone grigliato,
a grilled fillet served with braised endive, sundried tomatoes, and a light garlic sauce, is a good choice for anyone
craving the bounties of the sea. P.S. Single diners should ask
for the tiny table "on the piazza" and enjoy the warmth of
the neighborhood.

Resi's Bierstube

2034 West Irving Park

773-472-1749

$

Resi's is a snug little restaurant in St. Ben's with an out-
standing beer garden that delivers more old-fashioned German value than any other place in town; complete dinners,
excluding the schnitzels, hefty main dishes and two sides,
will set you back less than ten dollars. Choose from a variety of sausages or, if you're looking for something a little
out of the ordinary, fried liver cheese and potato salad. Wash
it all down with a selection from sixty bottled beers and
eight on tap. The place gets crowded with friendly regulars, and you may end up hoisting a stein inside with a
stranger—or maybe sharing your picnic table in the tree-
lined, lantern-lit beer garden with fellow diners who don't
know your name. When the mood is right, the solo diner

can actually enjoy the action at these communal tables. Service here is exceptionally friendly.

Shiroi Hana

3242 North Clark

773-477-1652

$ 🍴 🍴 🍴 🍴

👤 👤 👤   🍷 🍷

🏺 🏺 🏺 🏺 🏺   🏮 🏮

Crowded at all times, Shiroi Hana sets the Chicago standard for fresh, value sushi. While the restaurant has an extensive menu, it's the sushi combinations that keep the crowds spilling onto the sidewalk, like the $7.95 sushi deluxe (nine pieces and a roll), the California maki combo, and the all-veggie option with rolls wrapped in soy paper instead of seaweed. Service is efficient, although not necessarily warm, and single sushi mavens on a typically crowded night will find their best service and quickest seating at the sushi bar, although the restaurant will give you one of the tiny tables for two if you prefer.

Sipario Ristorante

3403 North Damen

773-248-7800/773-248-9523

$ $ 🍴 🍴

👤 👤   🍷 🍷 🍷 🍷

🏺 🏺   🏮 🏮 🏮 🏮

The restaurant sibling of Red Wine Bar, Sipario is a cavernous, windowless dining room dominated by a brick oven and graced with seemingly endless tables. Since it's always easy to land a spot here, neighborhood diners—in T-shirts or ties, solo or in packs—drop in for rich, creamy Italian food that packs a wallop for your arteries. While ravioli al *funghi* (ravioli stuffed with wild mushrooms) is served in a comparatively benign tomato cream sauce, gnocchi al pesto genovese sinks in pesto with a base of what feels like half-and-half. By contrast, seafood and mushroom risottos seem relatively light. A half-dozen simpler entrees range from chicken and salmon selections to veal and *filetto al balsamico*, a tenderloin sautéed in a balsamic vinaigrette reduction. The restaurant now has a separate entrance from Red; you'd think that while they were cutting a hole in a previously featureless outside wall they could have invested in some glass too. If they tire of the dark back room after eating, solo diners can move up to Red to relax and enjoy one of the wine bar's many wines by the glass.

Las Tablas

2965 North Lincoln

773-871-2414

$ $

In a city that enjoys its steaks, this Colombian steakhouse offers a slightly lighter and tangier option that will keep carnivores just as happy. The good-sized menu features variations on thin-cut, marinated steaks, and the *Picada Colombiana* offers a solo diner a great introduction to just about everything on the menu—chicken, rib-eye, pork, NY strip, sausage—except seafood. To offset all the protein, the butcher-block serving platters here are ringed in starch, including bread, yucca, potatoes, and plantain. Your only challenge at Las Tablas as a single diner may be eating it all yourself. If you have an aversion to communal tables, beware; there are very few small tables here, with most patrons seated at large "picnic tables" under the palm trees that decorate the room. Service can be a little slow when the place gets packed. Live music Fridays and Saturdays. BYOB.

Tibet Cafe
3913 North Sheridan
773-281-6666
$ 🍴 🍴 🍴
🕴 🕴 🕴
🍴 🍴 🍴 🍴   🎭 🎭 🎭 🎭 🎭

If you're seeking solitary peace and meditation, coupled with the traditional dishes of Central Asia, try Tibet Cafe. A small, serene storefront opened by two former Tibetan lamas, the blond-wood-paneled restaurant is decorated with seat cushions made of brightly colored, gilded sari fabrics. There are fascinating butter sculptures on the walls, creamy swirls of color traditionally made with yak butter and *tsampa* (roasted barley flour) that depict deities and Buddhist scenes, a uniquely Tibetan art that serves as a form of prayer in the monastery. You'll also notice prayer flags and, in a place of honor, a smiling picture of the Dalai Lama. Kick off your meal with a pot of *boe cha*, traditional Tibetan tea churned with light salt, butter, and milk. Dishes are modest in size, so a solo diner can comfortably taste several options, including *tsel momo*, the national dish of Tibet. *Momos* are pot-sticker look-alikes steamed and filled with mixed vegetables or fried (tsel momo *ngopa*) and served on a bed of shredded salad. More momos include those made with potatoes mixed into the vegetables (Tibet Cafe Special). Meat dishes feature beef versions of the momos, beef dumplings steamed (*shaymo*) or fried (*shaymo ngopa*). Other entree options include chicken and even seafood. Wind up dinner with *dysee*, sweetened rice studded with raisins mounded beside a warm yogurt. BYOB.

El Tinajon

2054 West Roscoe

773-525-8455

$

This brightly decorated neighborhood storefront is named after a handle-less clay pot traditionally used to hold fresh drinking water. The menu showcases dishes from the land of the Maya, which combined with Spanish influences to form Guatemalan cuisine. Lots of combination options allow solo diners a variety of tastes without needing to share with a dining partner. Guatemalan specialties— accompanied by frosty mugs of Gallo (Guatemalan beer)— include *Hilachas*, shredded beef and potatoes simmered in a "Creole" sauce, served with rice and *jocon cobanero*, chicken simmered in special green sauce. The menu's other offerings might sound similar to Mexican, but there's a Guatemalan twist on everything; chorizos, for example, are pork sausages prepared with Guatemalan spices and served with black beans, rice, broiled tomato sauce, and salad. Vegetarian dishes, along with pricier red snapper and shrimp dishes, are also available. Wash it all down with a frosty mug of Gallo (a Guatemalan beer) or an iced margarita. Small tables here are perfect for singles, but be prepared to have lots of people standing impatiently by the door watching you eat when the place gets crowded. Seats at the sidewalk cafe, bordered nicely with a hip-high picket fence, are sold out on nice days.

Victory's Banner
2100 West Roscoe
773-665-0227
$

If you think what the world needs now is more peace, love, and bliss burgers, check out Victory's Banner, where you and your spirit—no other dining companion required—may find inner strength. You'll also find a healthy meal at one of this storefront's small but brightly lit tables. Owner Pradhan Balter and his sari-clad staff subscribe to the teachings of Indian spiritual master Sri Chinmoy, who champions "a sincere inner life with an active outer life." With that in mind, the restaurant is vegetarian and offers to prepare dishes either for vegans or to meet special dietary requirements. Only hormone-free, free-range eggs are used in combination with soy sausage, tempeh "fakin' bacon," fresh fruit, and real whipped cream. The focus on health and spirituality doesn't dampen the popularity of chocolate chip pancakes or oat bran cakes served with toasted pecans, cinnamon-baked apples, and real maple syrup. Lunch features sandwiches, including a portabella mushroom wrap in a spinach tortilla with goat cheese and the "neatloaf" sandwich on hearth bread. Wash it all down with a bottomless mug of homemade Chai tea—smooth, creamy bliss in a cup. Not open for dinner.

Wishbone
3300 North Lincoln
773-549-2663
See page 16.

Zoom Kitchen
620 West Belmont
773-325-1400
See page 31.

NORTH

Albany Park, Andersonville, Argyle Street, Edgewater, Lincoln Square, Rogers Park, Uptown

AFRICANS, BOSNIANS, CHINESE, Croats, Filipinos, Germans, Greeks, Indians, Koreans, Lebanese, Native Americans, Norwegians, Orthodox Jews, Pakistanis, Serbs, Swedes, Thais, Vietnamese, and various Hispanic groups—the list goes on and on—the United Nations of Chicago is found on the North Side between Montrose and Howard Street, the city's northern border.

Chicago's northern neighborhoods, some of the most diverse in the city, are a melting pot of the North Side's original European settlers with those who later came from Asia, Africa, and Latin America. As a result, the city's northernmost eateries offer solo diners a global menu all within the small world of Chicago's far north side. Diners will find the Swedish meatballs and Middle Eastern delicacies of Andersonville, the dim sum and Vietnamese specialties of next-door neighbor Argyle Street, the jerk chicken and spicy goat stews of the numerous West Afrian and Afro-Caribbean eateries of East Rogers Park, the all-you-can-eat Indian buffets on Devon, the Korean banquets in Albany Park, and the year-round Oktoberfest celebration in Lincoln Square. It seems like all the tastes of the world can be sampled between Irving Park and Howard, most often in tiny storefronts that offer small tables just perfect for one.

With the exotic nature of much of the food on Chicago's North Side comes some culinary exploration for the solo diner. Outside of Andersonville and Lincoln Square, most North Side restaurants are casual storefronts. Many, however, make up for the lack of white-tablecloth elegance with a homey comfort that's a natural by-product of a family-run business, and it's just perfect for the solo diner. You won't need a passport to eat at any of them, but you will need to be ready for a little adventure.

Amitabul

6207 North Milwaukee

773-774-0276

$

Amitabul, which means "awakening," specializes in Korean and Tibetan Buddhist vegetarian food—glistening green piles of vegetable maki rolls, stacks of vegetable pancakes made with various grains, noodle dishes like Tibetan High Noon, whole wheat noodles and Korean vegetables with Tibetan curry and sesame oil, and soups like "Nine Ways to Nirvana," a whole wheat noodle soup with miso. The restaurant's a favorite place for solo diners who come from near and far to follow their own solitary culinary paths, and many are even on Amitabul meal plans. Diners can linger for hours over a bowl of "Dr. K's Cure-All," a spicy noodle soup, or *bi bim bop*, a Korean rice bowl that comes in various forms. The food at Amitabul is hot—from mildly spicy to hot with a capital "H"—and strictly vegan, with no dairy, even for coffee. Rice sake, beer, and wine are served, but the wines are plum, ginseng, or nine-grain.

Ann Sather
5207 North Clark
773-271-6677
See page 44.

Atlantique
5101 North Clark
773-275-9191

$ $

A former local bar, Atlantique is a bright and attractive neighborhood place in Andersonville. A casual atmosphere allows single diners to be comfortable, but there's nothing laid-back about Atlantique's food. Nominally a fish restaurant, Atlantique combines Asian, Italian, French, and even American flavors in a way that actually makes sense and tastes delicious—try the architectural anchovy salad of romaine hearts or the spectacular grilled ahi tuna served with seaweed salad, purple sticky rice, and lemongrass wasabi sauce. Bouillabaisse comes loaded with fish and tender seafood, while the seared dry pack scallops and lobster on mushroom polenta are made even richer by a Thai basil-infused lobster sauce. Even beef tenderloin with truffle-infused potatoes; braised veal tongue, bordelaise; and caramelized mango-cognac demi-glace are standouts at a place that considers itself a fish house.

La Bocca della Verita

4618 North Lincoln

773-784-6222

$ $

A long-time neighbor in Lincoln Square, La Bocca della Verita—The Mouth of Truth—spans three storefronts and offers the simple atmosphere of a small-town Italian trattoria. It's a casual place with small, well-spaced tables, good Italian cooking, and a nice selection of wines by the glass. Entrees pay tribute to Northern Italy's lighter culinary touch with choices like tender fettuccine tossed with baby artichokes and homemade gnocchi covered in a light tomato sauce, tender enough to melt in your mouth. They're just a starting point for a well-rounded menu that features tender veal scaloppine smothered in fresh vegetables and brandy, free-range chicken roasted with rosemary and garlic, and tender grilled octopus. Gelato fans, you're in luck; you'll find a rainbow of flavors to choose from, all homemade. Since it's next door to the Davis Theatre, this is a good option for a complete night out. If you don't live around here, it's well worth the drive to sample this place, even with the parking hassles.

Cafe Selmarie

2327 West Giddings

773-989-5595

$

A cadre of loyal locals frequents Cafe Selmarie for its light, eclectic meals, and the patrons often show up solo with a book or paper in hand. Tucked away on the plaza off Lincoln Avenue, this quiet spot contains a full-service bakery adjacent to a brightly lit dining room featuring the works of local artists. Entrees vary with the seasons and feature a daily pizza and quiche and meat and fish. A fall menu might include pan-seared Arctic char with sweet tomatoes and baby vegetables in a braised leek and white wine nage and a steak au poivre with celery root mash, chanterelles and a cognac demi-glace. The regular menu includes one of the most tender double-cut pork chops you'll ever bite into and chicken potpie. Take advantage of the patio dining on the peaceful plaza during Indian Summer. For those contemplating the end of solo dinerhood, the bakery does a brisk business in wedding cakes; Cafe Selmarie also hosts cake tastings in January and February.

Chicago Brauhaus

4732 North Lincoln
773-784-4444
$ $

Should you be in a mood to heft a stein solo in a friendly, festive atmosphere, the Lincoln Square landmark Chicago Brauhaus lets you celebrate Oktoberfest year-round. Although there's no way you'll be able to focus on reading anything here, you'll get plenty of entertainment from the traditional German oompah band that rocks here nightly, pumping out your favorite Bavarian drinking tunes and occasionally slowing it down with a little "Edelweiss." Like a Munich beer hall, this place is big, so you may feel a little swallowed up, and you might prefer to maintain a distance between your table and the action on the packed parquet dance floor, which offers great people watching. Dishes are typically German, big and heavy, with offerings like *königsberger klopse* (meatballs in caper sauce), Bavarian *leberkaese* à la Holstein (German fried potatoes, red cabbage, soup or salad), and various sausages served in pairs with a choice of potatoes, sauerkraut, or red cabbage, almost too much for one, so be prepared to take some home. Every fall, the Chicago Brauhaus also throws an Oktoberfest in Lincoln Square's main parking lot behind the restaurant.

Deluxe Diner

6349 North Clark (at Devon)

773-743-8244

$

When the rather shopworn Stacks and Steaks closed at this location, The Solo Diner lamented the loss of another staple where a table for one was all but guaranteed. But the tears were short-lived. Deluxe Diner has spiffed up the old place with chrome and red vinyl to create an instant classic that's as welcoming of singles as ever. You'll find gargantuan renditions of comfort foods like macaroni and cheese and hamburgers, along with spectacular breakfasts served twenty-four hours a day (with excellent egg dishes served in skillets). If the place fills up, solo diners can always grab a seat at the shiny counter. Servers are unbelievably warm—especially, it seems, to parties of one. P.S. Don't miss the indulgent ice-cream desserts.

La Donna

5146 North Clark

773-561-9400

$ $

âT âT âT

🍷 🍷

🍴 🍴 🍴

Y Y Y

♏

Cozy is the word for La Donna, a friendly little Anderson-ville trattoria that offers comfortable food in close confines. While portions are huge, dining space is tiny; not only are tables insufferably close together, but seats at those tables offer far less space than the average adult would seem to require. Solo diners will be glad to be alone. The menu describes itself as "creative Italian cuisine with a distinctive Roman accent"; specialties include a tender braised osso buco on saffron rice and the city's most decadent stuffed pasta dish, homemade pumpkin-filled ravioli "embraced" with a creamy balsamic vinegar sauce. Three different risot-tos are regular options, and the pride of the house is *zuppa di pesce*, a basin of linguine in tomato and garlic broth topped with a small mountain of seafood. Finish off with great tiramisù or a dish of *croccantino*, a light and airy fro-zen combination of mascarpone cheese, zabaglione, cracked caramel, and nuts drizzled with raspberry and cream sauce.

Grecian Taverna

4535 North Lincoln

773-728-1600

$

âT âT

🍷 🍷 🍷

🍴 🍴

Y Y

♏ ♏ ♏

Looking for an urban oasis to linger in? Lincoln Square's Grecian Taverna is a good option for the solo diner who wants to enjoy a Greek menu without feeling overwhelmed by the cavernous loud rooms, mediocre food, and general craziness typically found in Greektown. With Grecian Tavern's tree-studded patio, shady, tiled exterior, extensive menu of Greek specialties, and simple red-sauce Italian dishes, the restaurant offers Mediterranean tastes for anyone who wants to escape to the Aegean for lunch or dinner. Start your meal with a choice of one of over two dozen appetizers or taste a selection with either a hot or cold appetizer combo plate, which will give you lots to sample even without sharing with anyone else. Still hungry? Choose from one of the many charcoal-grilled lamb, pork, chicken, beef, or seafood dishes, including stingray or swordfish.

The Heartland Cafe

7000 North Glenwood

773-465-8005

$

The Heartland Cafe, a Rogers Park mainstay for nearly thirty years, is a destination that can occupy a solo diner for hours. The restaurant has a large room with lots of tables, so you'll never be hurried along, and the indoors is supplemented by one of the most colorful, spacious outdoor patios around, perfect for observing the ever interesting street activity of Rogers Park. Back inside, there's also live entertainment and a shop stocked with juices, books, and all sorts of garments and jewelry manufactured in Third World countries, all adding up to plenty of distractions as you while away some hours alone. And, you can pass your time in a healthy manner, which the Heartland's menu emphasizes with a large selection of poultry, fish, and seafood, as well as lentil and tempeh burgers and fried-bean plates. The Heartland has an extensive breakfast menu and, unlike many healthy places, a well-stocked bar. Breakfast is served daily until 3:00 P.M.

India Garden
2548 West Devon
773-338-2929

$

Not as fancy as its Devon neighbor Tiffin, but with significantly better food, India Garden offers one of the best all-you-can-eat buffets at both locations (see page 25 for Gold Coast address). It's also an ideal setup for solo diners. You get your very own steaming plate of fragrant tandoori chicken and another plate of soft, warm naan delivered for starters. Service is relatively attentive, even though they may only have to fill your water glass, while you do the rest of the work. Besides its extensive and fresh buffet, India House is known for its *tawa* and *kadhai* dishes. A tawa is an iron plate used to cook meats and breads over hot coals; the kadhai is an iron wok usually used to cook *mug* (chicken) and *goths* (meat) with chilies, tomatoes, fenugreek, and coriander over hot coals.

Kopi: A Traveler's Cafe
5317 North Clark
773-989-5674

$

This Andersonville coffeehouse has fought off Starbucks and other more commercial chains with a unique ambiance that keeps loyal patrons coming back. A tranquil place to relax for hours, Kopi offers numerous small, tightly packed tables, as well as an elevated platform in the front window where you can relax on pillows if you remove your shoes. Counter service is typical coffeehouse, but the food has a healthy and vegetarian bent. Desserts, such as various fruit pies, Bailey's Irish Cream cheesecake, and plush carrot cake, get high marks. Live music Monday and Thursday evenings. Coffee is sold in bulk, and Jalan Jalan, a boutique in the back of the cafe, sells travel books, ethnic clothing and jewelry, and other gifts from around the world. To add to the international atmosphere, clocks on the wall—no one looks at one here—track the time across global time zones, and the restrooms are marked "water closet." Bring a book and plan on spending some quality time here.

Lutz Continental Cafe & Pastry Shop

2458 West Montrose

773-478-7785

$

Try to pass by the immaculate bakery counters loaded with Chicago's creamiest napoleons, Sacher tortes, linzertortes, Grand Marnier tortes, and endless other temptations. Keep going beyond the elegant and very proper pink-tablecloth-clad dining room. Surprise: there's a sunny oasis back there. Bordered by tall hedges and ivy-covered walls and filled with a rainbow of wildflowers, the patio cafe at old world Lutz Continental Cafe is a slice of almost-suburban heaven, with its tables grouped around a gentle fountain in a reflecting pool carpeted with coins. It's a special "ladies who lunch" kind of place in good weather or bad, even for ladies who lunch alone. And what a lunch it is: Open-faced, Scandinavian-style sandwiches of Nova salmon, liver pâté, and Westphalian ham on German rye, assorted crepes, and an array of salads spanning from chicken to tuna to Caesar. Whichever salad you try, request the signature mustard-bacon dressing. Save room for dessert and coffee, which will be served to you in an individual pot on a doily-covered platter with two kinds of cream—liquid and whipped.

Moody's Pub

5910 North Broadway

773-275-2696

$

Revered citywide for its amazing half-pound hamburgers, Moody's has a rustic appeal and a warm welcome for solo diners. Dark wood paneling and tightly packed wooden tables are barely illuminated by the crackling fireplace, making this shadowy pub a snug retreat on a blustery winter's night. You can nurse a pint all throughout a solitary evening after you finish your Moody burger, but don't plan on reading in the murk here. With the onset of spring, move outside to Moody's two-tiered giant beer garden, with its ivy-clad walls and a ceiling of plush foliage, and enjoy one of the small round tables or a picnic bench.

Pasteur

5525 North Broadway

773-878-1061

$ $ 🍴 🍴 🍴 🍴

👷 👷 👷   🍸 🍸

🏺 🏺 🏺 🏺   ⛩ ⛩ ⛩

Pasteur is arguably the best-known Vietnamese restaurant in the city besides Le Colonial. The only problem for solo diners is that it's lushly romantic. Entering the restaurant is like stepping into a mansion in a scene from Marguerite Duras's *The Lover*, a shimmering trip back to the sophisticated decadence that marked the waning colonial days of French Indochina. Here in Chicago, that means a large, airy courtyard with lazy breezes from drop-ceiling fans caressing cushioned wicker armchairs pulled up to tables with snowy-white cloths. But if you can get beyond the lovey-dovey dining room ambience, you'll enjoy a meal of classic Vietnamese dishes that concentrate on texture, mixing cooked ingredients with raw, spicy or sour ingredients with mild, and cold foods with hot. For those who don't know what to order, stick with one of the many house specialties, including fragrant chicken sautéed with ginger in a sturdy brown clay pot (*ga kho gung*); fillets of catfish baked in the same clay pot and simmered with a concentrated sweet-tart glaze made from fish sauce, soy, and caramelized sugar; *bo cuon la lot*, delicate rolls of grilled beef wrapped in grape leaves and stuffed with minced chicken and shrimp; grilled scallops with sesame seeds and lemongrass sauce; and an East-meets-West combination of a seafood noodle bouillabaisse soup. As with most Asian restaurants, there's also a good selection of vegetarian dishes, including a combination of vegetables, tofu, and coconut milk.

Reza's
5255 North Clark
773-561-1898

Although there's plenty of Mediterranean-inspired competition in town, Reza's remains king of the castle when it comes to Middle Eastern. Both locations (see page 29 for Gold Coast address) are huge and bustling, so the solo diner is never begrudged a table, although you might feel swallowed up by the sheer size of the Andersonville location. Lots of veggie and meat combo options offer you plenty of opportunity to taste multiple things, without having to eat off of someone else's plate. With its nicely appointed rooms, value-priced meals, and free appetizers—not to mention some of the tallest, darkest, and handsomest waiters in Chicago—Reza's stands out from the crowd of local eating establishments that tend to be more Spartan storefronts.

Simplon Orient Express
4520 North Lincoln
773-275-5522/773-275-0033
$ $ 𝄞 𝄞 𝄞
🍴 🍴 🍴   Y Y
♟ ♟ ♟ ♟   ♏ ♏ ♏

If you're comfortable traveling on your own, you'll be entertained by an evening at Simplon Orient Express. Decorated like the inside of one of its famous namesake's sleeper cars, this Lincoln Square restaurant specializes in traditional dishes from the countries once visited by the legendary train as it steamed through the capitals of Europe to Istanbul. Starting in France with veal cordon bleu, the solo culinary traveler—given stomach capacity—can journey east through Switzerland for chicken sauté in wine sauce with a stop for holstein schnitzel in Germany. Then it's off to Austria for Wiener schnitzel, and south to Italy for spaghetti Milanese. A side trip takes you back up through Hungary then down to Serbia for numerous options. A stop in Greece for royal moussaka, and then it's back on track through Bulgaria (*natur* schnitzel) to the final destination. In Istanbul, Turkey, there's a finale of *sarma* (rolled sour cabbage leaves filled with veal, beef, and rice). Entrees are large and include appetizers and soup, so solo diners who want to experiment might choose the combination dish of *cevapcici* (sausages of veal, beef, and pork) and *raznjici* (beef kabobs) instead of trying to order numerous dishes. Open late with friendly service and rarely crowded, so you can make your trip on the Simplon Orient Express as long as you'd like.

Sun Wah Bar-B-Q Restaurant

1132–34 West Argyle

773-769-1254

$

Though Argyle Street is sometimes called New Chinatown, it's really better known for its Vietnamese and wider Asian influences. Still, Sun Wah is a real-deal Chinese treasure just west of the El stop. The decor here is nil, there's a little surface grime, and every place setting seems to include at least one not-quite-so-clean utensil. The food, however, offsets the last-chance atmosphere. Barbecue is the specialty; you'll have a chance to taste one of those gleaming carcasses hanging in the front window. There are lots of other tasty and unusual items on the menu. You can try simple dishes like rice *congee* (a simple porridge) or wonton soup, or venture further out to sea for steamed whitefish with salted olives and steamed fresh oysters served in the shell with black bean sauce.

Sunshine Cafe
5449 North Clark
773-334-6214
$ ♯ ♯ ♯

Everyone seems to know everyone else at Andersonville's tiny Sunshine Cafe, so you'll never actually feel alone at one of the ten tables in the wood-paneled dining room. Even if you're a stranger, you'll still get the same friendly treatment. Entrees include teriyaki, tempura, and sukiyaki. But there's a bonus for solo diners (and everyone adventuresome) in the abundance of small dishes, such as *goma-ae* (blanched spinach with sweet sesame sauce), *tsukemono* (pickled vegetables), and *gyoza* (pork dumplings). Inexpensive noodles are another ideal option here for solo diners; try the slurpy udon noodles, with meat or vegetables in a hearty broth, or the more unusual *zaru* soba, cold buckwheat noodles served with a fishy dipping sauce with *nori* (seaweed), green onions, and wasabi. BYOB.

Villa Kula
4518 North Lincoln
773-728-3114
$ $ ♯ ♯ ♯ ♯

Singularly one of the most serene places in the city, Villa Kula offers diners an elegant wood-and-glass interior with tile mosaics on the wall and a stupendous tea garden next door. Daily tea party service includes three-tiered towers of finger sandwiches, homemade scones with champagne strawberry jam and cream, and assorted desserts with lemon curd. Served tea for one or more which underscores Villa Kula's encouraging assumption that plenty of its guests are on their own. Individual plates of tea sandwiches, scones, or desserts are available, as is a full menu of pâtés, salads, and sandwiches, and a complete, high-end dinner menu. An assortment of tea ranges from black and green variations to oolong and tisane, and the staff will be happy to walk you through the nuances of each. Tea-tasting parties are held regularly, a perfect opportunity for independent learning. Live jazz and blues on Sunday evenings, no cover.

WEST

Avondale, Bucktown, Logan Square, Wicker Park, Ukrainian Village

BEGINNING IN THE early 1990s, the hippest stop on the CTA came to be found on the Blue Line at Damen, Milwaukee, and North avenues. Lincoln Park degenerated into post-collegiate sports bars and plastic trattorias, and eaters with attitude flocked to the gentrifying neighborhoods of Bucktown and Wicker Park. Which is part of the problem. Once the stomping grounds of starving artists, the area's resident tattoos and body piercings mingle increasingly with yuppies and suburbanites as the cutting edge of nightlife, both for music and dining, has moved to 2000 West. Beautiful people and the in crowd are doing Damen. From Webster south to Division, Damen Avenue is packed with culinary trendsetters feeding on Italian, Mexican, French, South American, various Asian, and global mishmashes of all of the aforementioned at restaurants that have copped enough attitude to freeze a solo diner in his tracks.

These days, if you want to find a place where you can stake out a comfy table and not worry about the SRO crowds of the underdressed and fashion forward, you just might need to venture out of Wicker Park and Bucktown, to similarly trendy but less crowded alternatives in East Village and Ukrainian Village, and maybe even Humboldt Park. North of Bucktown in Latino Logan Square and Polish Avondale, you'll still find plenty of family-run establishments that offer you numerous options to dine on interesting dishes on your own for a relatively small price while lingering until you finish your book (and maybe even start another).

A Tavola
2152 West Chicago
773-276-7567
$ $

Once the home of Soul Kitchen, A Tavola is so small, you'll be glad you're dining solo. Its crisp white walls are lined with black-and-white photos, and a swooping red velvet curtain provides the sole splash of color at the entrance. You won't find grandma's noodles and red sauce at this tiny Italian restaurant in Ukrainian Village whose small seasonal menu changes weekly. Starting options might include grilled eggplant rolls filled with Gorgonzola and grilled beef tenderloin with chard, or plump gnocchi with pesto sauce—rumored to be the best in the city. Roasted chicken with polenta or garlicky spinach and sliced potatoes grilled with Parmesan and rosemary are both standouts too, as are assorted risottos. Finish with caramelized baked apple tart and flourless Swiss chocolate-and-hazelnut torte. Small but well-chosen wine list.

Bar Louie

1704 North Damen

773-645-7500

See page 19.

Bite Cafe

1039 North Western

773-395-BITE (2483)

$

Adjoining Ukrainian Village's Empty Bottle, where you can indulge in some postdining progressive music and a beer, Bite is a cramped storefront with character and creative food at prices that don't, well, bite. Tables are close together, and there's plenty of Wicker Park attitude here from the staff, but it's directed equally at singles and groups. Still, you might feel pressured to eat and run when the place gets busy, so dine strategically. The regular menu, written on elementary school workbooks, is primarily sandwiches and pastas, but the real draw here is the changing nightly dinner specials. A some-time option, the Indian sampler with eggplant and vegetable curry, is an artistic version of what's offered up at California and Devon. Chicken with cilantro sauce, rice, and grilled potatoes; leg of lamb with red pepper sauce and ratatouille; and miso-marinated shark with rice, sprouts, spinach, and cucumbers can all be enjoyed without breaking a twenty-dollar bill. Bite serves a great brunch on the weekends. BYOB.

Bongo Room

1470 North Milwaukee

773-489-0690

$

The Bongo Room offers one of the city's best reasons to leave the comfort of the sheets at an early hour. With an ever-changing seasonal menu executed with creativity and flair, the Bongo Room turns breakfast and lunch into a decadent culinary affair. Crowds line up here before the door opens; singles wait like everyone else and will be rewarded with a small table, while those who consent to slide into a seat at the bar will be welcomed with unusual warmth by these harried servers. The food is the other pay-off. Chocolate tower French toast, stuffed with maple mascarpone, drizzled with banana crème brûlée sauce, and garnished with bananas and shaved chocolate; the rock shrimp and asparagus benedict; and pancake options like carrot cake flapjacks with warm cream cheese icing and cinnamon crème anglaise and Butterfinger banana hotcakes with Valrhona chocolate crème anglaise and fresh bananas are just some of the Bongo Room's seasonal treats. Not open for dinner.

Le Bouchon

1958 North Damen

773-862-6600

$ $

For years, Le Bouchon, which means "the cork" in French, has been the most authentically French of Chicago's bistros. Located in Bucktown, the city's left bank, the restaurant's often haughty waiters serve French classics to crowds that continue to pack its intimate, lace-curtained space. Waits are long, even with reservations, so dine strategically. You may be glad you don't have to share your tiny table with a companion, but you'll be hard-pressed to relax and read here on a Saturday night. While steak *frites* with a dollop of herb butter and hangar steak with wine sauce are the menu's anchors, Le Bouchon also cooks up homey, earthy versions of old favorites like escargots, kidneys in mustard sauce, rabbit, and other classics, as well as a number of fresh fish options. P.S. Nonsmokers beware. Pervasive cigarette smoke here is another authentic French touch.

Cafe Bolero

2252 North Western

773-227-9000

$

A short walk from the relatively new City North 14 Cinema, friendly Cafe Bolero is a Cuban eatery well-positioned to be the front end of an evening's entertainment. A longtime neighborhood option on the northwest edge of Bucktown, this place is popular among Latino locals from the Humboldt Park and Logan Square enclaves next door. It's also a warm spot for any solo diner to stop in for a generous meal and a cup of dark Cuban coffee. Appetizers include ham croquettes, stuffed potato balls, and meat-stuffed plantains, all of which can be sampled by ordering the special combo platter. The menu also features hearty sandwiches like the ham, pork, and cheese *medianoche* ("midnight") sandwich. Many entrees, like *boliche* (stuffed beef roast) and chicken fricassee, are accompanied by beans and plantains. Opt for a *mojito Cubano*, a mixture of rum and freshly crushed mint leaves—or any other Cuban beverage—over wine here. In season, outdoor sidewalk seating has some candlelit ambiance and is a good place to sip sangria and relax amidst the chatter in Spanish.

Caffe De Luca

1721 North Damen

773-342-6000

$

For a neighborhood that prides itself on being at the core of Chicago's Left Bank, it's surprising how few coffeehouse hangouts Bucktown offers solo diners. Enter Caffe De Luca. With its unfinished floors and terra-cotta half-walls studded with grills and windows, this place offers a romantic setting reminiscent of an ancient Tuscan alleyway. Like most coffeehouses, De Luca serves a wide assortment of beverages, muffins, light bites, and desserts, including an assortment of gelatos. Besides its Renaissance atmosphere, what distinguishes De Luca from the average coffee bar is the abundance of more filling options; you'll find cold and grilled Italian sandwiches made with combinations of grilled eggplant, red pepper, prosciutto, cappicola, mozzarella, and basil, along with cheese plates and three kinds of pâté with crostini (triangular toast points). Pet-owning solo diners, rejoice. Even your best friend can enjoy the visit, and dogs get free panini biscuits. All prices are translated into Italian lira—at a pretty good rate. Open late.

Club Lucky
1824 West Wabansia
773-227-2300
$ $

The food and service at this 1940s-style Bucktown supper club/cocktail lounge are significantly overrated. The restaurant, however, remains a neighborhood mainstay, where plenty of solo diners drop in for a drink and dinner. Club Lucky, however, is often crowded, and if you feel like sipping a signature shaken-not-stirred martini with a hand-stuffed olive and tackling a huge plate of traditional red sauce Sicilian on your own, be prepared to wait for your glutinous dining experience. Pastas and desserts are all homemade; portions guarantee you'll be taking some home. Aluminum and glass light fixtures in the dining room are replicas of pieces from the Empire State Building when it was built, and the bar area is a replica of the original 1938 Club Lucky's space. Service can be spotty, and it's not going to get any better for you when you're on your own.

Czerwone Jabluszko (The Red Apple)
3121–23 North Milwaukee
773-588-5781

6474 North Milwaukee
773-763-3407
$

The daily buffet tables at this Polish restaurant provide what may be Chicago's best pig-outs for the dollar. You get all you can eat for $4.50 at lunch, $4.95 at dinner weekdays, and $5.95 at dinner weekends. With hot and cold buffets on room-length tables groaning under the weight of innumerable delicacies, you'll be glad you're alone, so that you can eat (and eat, and eat) without being self-conscious. Try to remain calm as you attack the salads, desserts, and assorted traditional Polish dishes and sides, including sauerkraut, stuffed cabbage, dumplings, roasts, sausages, goulash, cheese blintzes, potato pancakes, fritters, assorted pork parts (hocks and snouts), baked apples, and so much more. You can stay all day if you like, and keep eating. The Red Apple's buffet also includes a beverage, soup, and ice cream, which you have to request from your waitperson. There's a fully stocked grocery store next door, in case you just didn't get enough and need to take some home.

Earwax

1564 North Milwaukee

773-772-4019

$ 🍴 🍴 🍴

Though the food here excels, the emphasis is on coffee drinks, including the bottomless cup of regular. As a result, patrons tend to linger, and tables are more often occupied by solo diners than by couples or groups. The service, however, doesn't always match the quality of the food. It would be a compliment to call the help better than grudging; some put it down to Wicker Park attitude. But if a surly waitstaff doesn't bother you, you'll enjoy a menu that is several steps beyond the typical coffeehouse's, including an extensive array of sandwiches and specials oriented to the healthy and multiethnic vegetarian. A Middle Eastern plate, portabella sandwich, and a BBQ sloppy seitan sandwich or burrito all rock. The tofu scramble served with potatoes and a bagel is a popular morning option, and Earwax is also open late. P.S. Earwax's cafe is combined with a video store, giving a new meaning to dinner and a movie. BYOB.

Hi Ricky Asian Noodle Shop & Satay Bar

1852 West North

773-276-8300

$

The Hi Rickys are bright, open storefronts that serve a variety of Asian cuisines at practically Third World prices. Each location has lots of small tables, as well as counter seating, making Hi Ricky a good option for an inexpensive solo meal in a lively environment. Noodles, rice, soup, and curry selections feature options from China, Thailand, Vietnam, Singapore, Malaysia, Indonesia, and even Burma. The Malaysian *hokkien* noodles, Filipino *pancit canton* noodles, Indonesian *bakmi goreng*, Cambodian fried rice, and Peking duck illustrate the range of national dishes available. Have a Thai iced coffee or a ginger beer—or something more potent—to wash it all down.

Hilary's Urban Eatery

1500 West Division

773-235-4327

$

Once consisting almost entirely of counter seats, Hilary's opened up a back room several years ago to better accommodate groups. Luckily, plenty of counter space remains, and Hilary's is still a favorite of solo diners. Service is friendly and fast—it's just a reach over the counter to refill your cup or to serve you a warm slice of homemade pie à la mode. Serving all-day breakfasts, lunch, and dinner at the eastern edge of Wicker Park, Hilary's offers an eclectic mix of healthy options and comfort food like rib eye steak and eggs, barbecued beef, crab cakes, salmon cakes in Louis sauce, and—some swear—the best homemade macaroni and cheese in the city. Breakfast features Frisbee-sized specialty pancakes, ranging from oatmeal banana to spicy pumpkin raisin, and the six-dollar Pan Special delivers three hot cakes, three eggs, two sausage patties, and two strips of bacon. P.S. A jar of jelly beans graces every table and is only a reach away from any counter seat. BYOB.

Irazu

1865 North Milwaukee

773-252-5687

$ 🍴 🍴 🍴 🍴

🔥

👤 👤 👤 👤 👤   🪑 🪑

Irazu, originally a fast-food stand, is a friendly, self-serve Costa Rican oasis on a still-developing stretch of Milwaukee Avenue between Bucktown and Humboldt Park that attracts patrons of all types in all sizes in all size parties—from yuppie couples living in expensive new lofts south on Milwaukee to kids from the neighborhood to the west to solo diners who have a hankering for a giant, spicy, Central American–style chicken burrito the Costa Rican steak dinner, or a cilantro-and-pepper-laden steak taco. Breakfast options include huevos rancheros, huevos con chorizo or gallo pinto, and white rice with black beans and eggs or plantains. On a nice day, you can relax on the patio, admire the scenery, and sip a refreshing tropical fruit shake (fifteen different flavors, with or without milk). Although a dining room was finally opened several years ago to give patrons an eat-in alternative to the patio in less accommodating weather, seating is still limited; so if you want to eat in, you're actually much better off as a party of one than a party of six. Specials, including pork chops with rice and beans, are all less than ten dollars. BYOB. Cash only.

Kaleidoscope

1560 North Damen

773-489-0803

$

In the shadow of the Damen Avenue stop on the Blue Line El, this minuscule breakfast and lunch place serves a cadre of loyal locals who wouldn't go anywhere else for their omelets, pancakes, and burgers, all honestly prepared and generous. The room itself is college-dorm basic; the real treat is grabbing one of the plastic chairs outside in warm weather and watching the passing parade. You'll always see a small army of solo diners here on any given day, paying more attention to their reading than their surroundings or food. Servers are uniformly friendly and talkative, lighting inside is terrific. P.S. Open only until 3:00 P.M. seven days.

Leo's Lunchroom

1809 West Division

773-276-6509

Long before Wicker Park was trendy, there was Leo's. A fiercely independent dive decorated with postcards and other paraphernalia, Leo's features a half-dozen tables, a lengthy counter, and no air-conditioning. A multiethnic array of appetizers and changing chalkboard of entrees is served—soba noodles, wild mushroom risotto, sesame chicken wings, chicken *tagine* with couscous, sea scallops with *achiote* sauce, chicken with Thai red curry and yams. Alcohol is BYOB (there is no corking fee, and a liquor store is right across the street) and is served in plastic teacups, which says something about the attentive but no-frills service. Singles and groups all get packed in here. You should sit at the counter if you want to read and linger. Nice backyard patio for clement weather.

Lula Cafe
2537 North Kedzie
773-489-9554
lulacafe.com

It's hard to find a coffeehouse or cafe of character these days where you can linger and fill yourself up with more than a muffin or a scone. But Logan Square's Lula Cafe delivers with a variety of sandwiches and pastas, many of which feature Asian or Middle Eastern accents. Plump sandwiches on bakery-quality bread range from updated standards, like roast turkey with avocado and smoky chili aioli, to exotica like *tineka*, a spicy peanut butter served on multigrain bread with tomato, cucumber, and Indonesian sweet soy sauce. Other light bites include a feta cheese plate and sesame noodles. Entrees, served after 5:00 P.M., range from penne arrabbiata with tequila-lime tomato sauce and pasta *yiayia*, hollow macaroni with Moroccan cinnamon and brown butter sauce, to pan-fried herb chicken and Moroccan chickpea–sweet potato *tagine* with Saigon cinnamon and couscous. Brunch, featuring brioche French toast and a tofu scramble, is also very popular. In the tradition of many coffeehouses, art is still honored, with local artists' works on display and music in the evening. You'll catch many of those same artists enjoying a couple of hours by themselves at a table for one.

Pacific Cafe

1619 North Damen
773-PACIFIC (722-4342)
$

Located in a tiny, converted produce market, Pacific Cafe is a welcome "budget buy" in the midst of Bucktown/Wicker Park's trendiness and high prices, and its casualness also makes it a good destination for a solo diner, where many of the other local options offer too much of a scene for a single eater to feel comfortable. Pacific Cafe serves Thai, Japanese, and Vietnamese dishes. There's a full sushi menu, with some innovative options, along with representative appetizers from all three cuisines. Entrees include a long list of noodle dishes and curries. Food is served on brightly colored dishes marked by Pacific Rim designs. Service is extremely hospitable but can be slow.

Penny's Noodle Shop
1542 North Damen
773-394-0100
See page 59.

Pontiac Produce and Cafe
1531 North Damen
773-252-7767
$

Located in a former mechanic's garage, the Pontiac Produce and Cafe affords a premium hangout opportunity for solo diners. You'll find a sun-splashed parking lot of tables filled with hip loungers scattered in front of an airy interior with cool, shady booths. You'll notice them sipping fruit smoothies and generally being as sedentary as possible. The menu assembles and reassembles key ingredients like mozzarella, tomato, basil, red peppers, balsamic vinegar, and bread to create its two dozen offerings like salads, panini, and focaccia. Service is full of Wicker Park attitude. If you're in a hurry, opt for the "to go" counter. A DJ plays Saturday, Monday, and Wednesday after 10:00 P.M.

Rambutan
2049 West Division
773-772-2727
$ $

Named for a white-fleshed fruit found in Southeast Asia, Rambutan highlights the sweet-and-sour, tangy-and-spicy flavors of the Philippines. Portions are deliberately small to encourage exploration so solo diners can sample quite a range without needing someone else to share with. While some dishes will be familiar to fans of Asian cuisine— *lumpia* Shanghai (cigar-thin egg rolls), caramelized five-spice ribs, and rice-and-egg *pancit* noodles with Chinese sausage, chicken, shiitake mushrooms, and julienne root vegetables in oyster sauce—others are more exotic. The Solo Diner had never before sampled two different *camarones* (tiger shrimp) offerings, the *at gata*, sautéed in coconut milk and balanced delicately atop roasted garlic and coconut mashed potatoes, or *camaron rebosado*, fried and spiced with Asian mustard and served with a pickled green papaya salad. Chicken adobo, the Filipino national dish of soy-marinated chicken braised with rice wine, ginger, and garlic is a good bet, as is coriander-crusted beef in spicy black bean barbecue sauce. Finish off with almond *leche* flan or a *halo-halo*, a Filipino blizzard. Traditional Filipino dim sum brunch on Sundays from 9:30 A.M. to 2:00 P.M. P.S. The tables are relatively close in a small space here, so it may be tough to linger and read when the place gets crowded. Dine strategically.

Rinconcito Sudamericano

1954 West Armitage
773-489-3126
$ $

This unpretentious Bucktown storefront is Chicago's best option for Peruvian cuisine, and the high-quality fare more than makes up for slow service. Rinconcito Sudamericano is bright and spacious, so solo diners will also feel comfortable among the local families who like to gather here. Try the *arroz con mariscos* (Peruvian paella) and the house specialty of *aji de gallina* (shredded chicken in a nut cream with potatoes, Peruvian spices, and rice). A large menu offers plenty of chicken, game, and seafood options. Be sure to save room for a side dish of plantains. Beers go better with most of the food than wine. P.S. Be prepared to haul home a big doggy bag; portions here are huge.

Riverside Deli

1656 West Courtland
773-278-DELI (3354)
$

A 100-year-old family store and adjoining multiroom structure decorated in nostalgia with a secluded tree-shaded deck, Bucktown's Riverside Deli serves sandwiches daily and a stupendous, gut-filling, all-you-can-eat Sunday brunch. For $9.95, you can fill up from sideboards groaning under an eclectic array of cereals, breads, fruit, and cold salads; hot entrees that range from pancakes and eggs Benedict to cheese blintzes with fruit and fried tamales; and then finish it all off with a trip to the dessert room featuring elaborate sweets as well as some individually packaged Hostess treats. The staff isn't pressured by the crowds and will leave you alone as long as you keep eating. Hide yourself away in one of the Riverside's many nooks, and dig in at your leisure. Cash only. Open until 8:00 P.M. during the summer; otherwise closes by 4:00 P.M. (except Sundays, 3:00 P.M.).

Sak's Ukrainian Village Restaurant
2301 West Chicago
773-278-4445
$

Dining solo and looking for a taste of old Chicago? Try Sak's, one of the last remaining traditional restaurants in Ukrainian Village. Comfortably casual, somewhat dim, Sak's is the kind of place where you can hang out for the entire evening—you may need to just to digest its heavy dinners. Entrees all come with soup, salad, potato, and dessert. Choices range from *kapusta* and *kobassa* (sauerkraut with Ukrainian sausage), to *helubtsy* (cabbage rolls with meat and rice) in either a mushroom gravy or tomato sauce, to *plyatsky* (potato pancakes). *Varenyky*, Ukrainian dumplings similar to pierogis, are stuffed with meat, cheese, sauerkraut, or potato and smothered in either mushroom gravy or hot butter with bacon bits. Chicken Kiev, schnitzel, and even hamburgers are available for the less adventurous. Want it all? Try the "family feast" for $8.95 a person—available for singles as well. It seems to include a taste of almost everything on the menu. Top off your dinner with homemade apple pie, which at Sak's is closer to a multilayer apple torte than to a slice of Mom's American version. Rinse it all down with a cup of Ukrainian coffee which can be enhanced with something special from the bar.

Silver Cloud Bar & Grill
1700 North Damen
773-489-6212

$

Bucktown's Silver Cloud keeps to its quiet neighborhood self while establishments a few doors down attract long lines of "see-and-be-seen" wannabes. Like its cozy, comfortable interior, the Silver Cloud serves cozy comfort food, allowing solo diners to tuck themselves in and linger through the evening with a hot meal and a cold beer (a dozen are on tap). It's a snug, albeit dimly lit, room with comfy booths, a long bar, and a very eclectic bag of patrons—The Solo Diner's seen everyone from neighborhood regulars and cops on break to poseurs who drift a few doors too far north (more often when the sidewalk tables are out during nice weather). Small bites, sandwiches, and pastas are available, along with full-blown entrees, or "good eats," like chicken potpie or Grandma's meat loaf, served with mashed potatoes and green beans.

Smoke Daddy

1804 West Division

773-772-MOJO (6656)

$

"Rhythm & Barbecue" combine seven days a week at this Wicker Park institution, where a neon "WOW" flashes over the door, and the same exclamation is in the flavor of the food. There's no cover for the hot music available nightly with the hot sauce, and the casual neighborhood attitude of Smoke Daddy makes it a good option for a solo diner to enjoy some classic Chicago food and blues. In fact, the

Solo Diner's noticed lots of neighborhood regulars here on their own and in groups. Smoke Daddy cooks up peppery "Memphis-Texarkana" pig parts, spare ribs, tips, turkey, and beef brisket, along with specials like steak and shrimp done just right in a "smokehouse" pit barbecue oven from Texas that weighs nearly a ton. A combination of burning wood, fans, and stone embedded in the door of the pit is designed to duplicate the flavor of an old-fashioned brick barbecue pit. Vegetarians can opt for the Smoke Daddy sauce on a chargrilled veggie burger or defer with macaroni and cheese and a side of greens. Attempt to leave room for daily dessert treats like Key lime pie and cheesecake. P.S. A hand sink in the back makes it easy to clean up after your feast.

Toast
2046 North Damen
773-772-5600
See page 30.

Zoom Kitchen
1646 North Damen
773-278-7000
See page 31.

SOUTH

Bridgeport, Chinatown, Hyde Park

THE SOUTH SIDE of Chicago is, potentially, the baddest part
of town for solo diners, unless you're willing to work a little harder. The student population at the University of Chicago, as well as a professional contingent taking advantage
of some classic housing, ensures that Hyde Park and Ken-
wood offer some interesting dining options, many of which
are good finds for solo diners.

   Chicago's Chinatown is overrated compared to those of
other major cities, and the restaurants tend to be crowded,
noisy, and often, none too spic-and-span. Unless you've
really got a hankering for some dim sum, skip Chinatown
and explore southwest into Bridgeport, where you can combine an ethnic meal with a White Sox game, or head farther
south into either Marquette Park for some Lithuanian fare.
As expected, some of the best soul food in the city is found
on the South Side, as are Latino options in gentrifying
Pilsen and Little Village. Heart of Italy, centered around
24th Place and Oakley Avenue, offers a warm Northern Ital-

ian option to the Southern Italian typically served at the better known restaurants on Taylor Street.

There are plenty of tables for one in some of the oldest neighborhoods in the city. It may just take some looking.

Calypso
5211C South Harper
773-955-0229
$ $

There's not a huge number of decent, sit-down dining options for parties of any size in Hyde Park, but for a taste of the Caribbean, head to Calypso. Opened by the owners of Dixie Kitchen & Bait Shop right next door, Calypso serves the spices of Jamaica and its neighboring islands in a bright, playful water wonderland setting. Orders are generous enough to overwhelm anyone dining alone, but the servers, as friendly and warm as the islands, will encourage you to take home the extras. For those who don't like doggy bags, half orders make the menu more manageable for solo diners, and the half order of curried chicken, spicy-sweet with green apples, grapes, and raisins over white rice, is a good choice; as is the half order of house-smoked baby back ribs, which feature a barbecue sauce with just a taste of tropical fruit.

Dixie Kitchen & Bait Shop
5225 South Harper
773-363-4943
$

Both the Hyde Park and Evanston Dixie Kitchen locations
deliver tasty Southern-style cooking and Southern-style hospitality, even to solo diners, many of whom you'll see lingering here, as you might expect at an inexpensive place in
a university community. While both restaurants are decorated with "truck stop, gas station" decor and kitschy mem-
orabilia on the walls, the menu delivers the real thing. Fried
green tomatoes and various po' boys with rémoulade are traditional tasty fixin's, as is the catfish fillet. The "Southern
Sampler" is also a good option for a solo diner who wants
to taste everything. Hot cornmeal johnnycakes start each
meal instead of a basket of bread. Wash it all down with a
Blackened Voodoo beer.

Healthy Food
3236 South Halsted
773-326-2724
$

Healthy Food, open since 1938 and the oldest Lithuanian
restaurant in the city, is located just west of Comiskey Park.
The restaurant, which ironically serves huge, inexpensive
portions of artery-clogging Lithuanian and Eastern European specialties seven days a week for prices that draw loyal
locals, as well as patrons who drive in from well outside the
neighborhood. Its Old World, casual dining area is a comfortable place for a solo diner to relax at one of the four-
teen tables or counter and digest a heavy meal of comfort
food. Homemade Lithuanian specials include *blynai*, Lithuanian pancakes with a dozen different kinds of fillings
including *vsysniu* (sour cherry) and *spanguoliu* (cranberry);
koldunai, (boiled meat or cheese dumplings served with sour

cream and bacon); *kugelis*, (Lithuanian dumplings); and roast half duck. Meals are accompanied by fresh-baked Lithuanian rye or pumpernickel. All these Lithuanian favorites include dessert—a choice of Jell-O with a swirl of whipped cream or *kolacky*, traditional fruit-filled pastries. No alcohol. Cash only.

Penang

2201 South Wentworth

312-326-6888

$ 🍴 🍴 🍴 🍴

👤 👤   🍸 🍸

🏮 🏮 🏮 🏮   🏮 🏮

Unlike its swankier cousins in New York City, Chicago's Penang in Chinatown is relatively dumpy. It's also so cavernous you may feel lost on your own, even at one of the smaller tables of four. On top of that, your servers may have trouble finding you, especially on a busy weekend night. But the ordeal's often worth it for the food. Penang specializes in Southeast Asian cuisines with an emphasis on Malaysian dishes, while a sushi bar, Indian accents, and Chinese influences give the restaurant a little extra Pan-Asian spice. As starters, *roti canai* and *roti telur* are light, Indian-inspired breads that taste bland alone but make perfect scoops for curries. House specials like *kambing rendang* (lamb curry in eleven different spices), *sambal sotong* (squid in lemongrass and shrimp paste), and *sambal ikan bilies* (anchovies in chilies and tamarind sauce), all showcase multiple layers of spices and seasonings. Finish off with an ice *kachang*, an Everest of shaved ice with beans, black jelly, and rose syrup that makes a great fire extinguisher to dinner's fiery flavors.

EVANSTON AND
THE NORTH SHORE

EVANSTON—IT'S NOT just for kids anymore. Once a gas-
tronomic desert, seemingly catering solely to the cash-
pressed student population with almost no dining options
bridging the culinary gap between McDonald's and Buf-
falo Joe's and the now long-gone, three-star Café Proven-
cal, Evanston has experienced a dining renaissance. From
make-your-own stir-fry and relaxing coffee shops to perky
bistros and casual sit-downs to higher-end options—even
a Wolfgang Puck's Cafe—Evanston now offers numerous
eating opportunities of all types that'll make a solo diner
comfortable.

Diners who enjoy a drink with dinner have also seen
Evanston's attitude toward the grape (and the hop) change
slowly over the years. As those who study local history
know, absolute temperance was repealed in 1972, allowing
Evanston's first legal beer to be served in restaurants. The
town's nightlife has gradually improved, and today, there's
a good selection of places besides the Orrington Hotel that

serve alcohol, even a number of restaurants that stake their reputations on their wine cellars.

Evanston—it's not just a place to go to school anymore. Dial 847 for a reservation, or just pop up for a visit.

Bar Louie
913 North Milwaukee, Wheeling
847-279-1199
See page 19.

Big Bowl
215 Parkway Drive, Lincolnshire
847-808-8880

1950 East Higgins Road, Schaumburg
847-517-8881
See page 20.

Blind Faith Cafe
525 Dempster
847-328-6876
$

The Blind Faith Cafe serves ethnic-influenced vegetarian and vegan favorites ranging from barbecue seitan sandwiches to Japanese-influenced macrobiotic plate, an enjoyable dish of brown rice topped with shiitake mushroom sauce, vegetable and bean of the day, steamed kale vinaigrette, sea vegetable, cup of miso soup, and a pickle. Light entrees include pastas; healthy Mexican bean tostadas and chili enchiladas; and various combinations of seitan, tofu, and tempeh. The restaurant's bakery turns out plenty of fresh vegan and nonvegan options for dessert or to take home. Like any inexpensively priced option in a college town, you'll find plenty of solo diners, and Blind Faith's cozy dining room, decorated with plants and hanging quilts on the wall, makes it a particularly warm place to hang out and indulge your health over a newspaper or a book. Wine and beer are served.

Campagnola

815 Chicago
847-475-6100
$ $ $

There's no place better for solo diners to splurge in Evanston than this smooth, sophisticated, but relaxed winner. Though lighting could be better, the welcome, service, and food could not; The Solo Diner has had few experiences where an entire restaurant's team worked together so harmoniously. Even better, chef/owner Michael Altenberg's food has only improved since Campagnola opened in 1996. There's a tasting menu as well as à la carte options. The Solo Diner recently savored starters of ahi tuna tartar with hearts of palm, avocado, and salsa and a rich duck foie gras with black mission fig. Entrees are close to perfect, including pan-seared Hawaiian silver snapper with vegetables, a succulent whole loup de mer baked in rock salt, and a lusty wild boar chop. Desserts, like sponge cake with mascarpone, are simple and delicious. Terrific selection of wines by the glass; full menu served at the bar. P.S. The recently opened Trattoria Campagnola offers a more casual atmosphere and menu downstairs, while Campagnola's more intimate dining room operates upstairs.

Dixie Kitchen & Bait Shop

825 Church Street, Evanston

847-733-9030

See page 106.

Lulu's

626 Davis

847-869-4343

$

Because of Lulu's, cash-poor students don't have to be faced with a choice between wings or Big Macs. On their own at a small, sunny table or in groups, students and locals flock to Lulu's, which offers "dim sum and then sum" with bright decor and no-frills style. Lulu's serves a selection of "fusion Asian," including dumplings and other "small eats," soups, salads, and stir-fry. Dim sum is a big hit here, especially on Monday evenings and Sunday afternoons when it's a $10.95 all-you-can-eat affair. Entrees play on a range of Japanese, Chinese, Thai, and Vietnamese themes. The Vietnamese rice noodle salad topped with grilled beef and a spring roll is a big hit, as are other entrees such as jumbo shrimp and mixed veggies with Thai panang coconut curry and rice. Try the won ton sundae for dessert. Beer, wine, and sake.

The Stained Glass Bistro

1735 Benson

847-864-8600

$ $ $

A serious dining establishment lurks behind a casual wine-bar facade here. The menu is solid and honest, with earthy ingredients in intriguing combinations. Braised rabbit in red mole sauce with butternut squash makes an inviting starter; likewise the grilled baby octopus salad with beets and tomatoes. Among the entrees, the New Zealand lamb rack with white bean puree and the baked Alaskan halibut with squash custard stand out. The pièce de résistance for solo diners here is the choice of thirty-two wines by the glass, some of which come from the dozen or so wine racks by the entrance; most of them are available for purchase and even delivery. Lighting is adequate; service is very accommodating.

Unicorn Cafe
1723 Sherman
847-332-2312
$

Since it opened in 1991, the Unicorn has attracted a steady stream of regulars drawn as much by the counter staff's warmth and hospitality as the fifty-cent coffee refills and good, cheap snacks and sandwiches. Northwestern students swarm here, seeming to prefer it over the coffee chains that have colonized Evanston these last few years. Do like the locals—buy a few papers, pull up a chair, and sip the hours away. P.S. Excellent lighting.

HOTEL RESTAURANTS

HOTEL RESTAURANTS HAVE always been havens for solo diners. A preponderance of business travelers has always meant at least a couple of solo diners in any hotel restaurant. But hotel dining used to mean generic, overpriced food in glorified coffee shops.

Not anymore. Today, you'll find some of Chicago's most talked-about restaurants inside their lodging properties. Locals are even partaking shoulder-to-shoulder with the tourists.

On the one hand, that's good news if you're seeking a table for one. The excitement in hotel kitchens means standards keep rising. The downside is that the hotter they get, many hotel dining rooms become less hospitable to solo diners (try getting noticed at the self-consciously hip NoMi in the new Park Hyatt). The following are a few choices where The Solo Diner was mostly received as a welcome guest rather than an unwanted pest.

Atwood Cafe

Hotel Burnham
1 West Washington
312-368-1900
$ $ $

With its blue-and-gold motif, and light and dark woods, the eighty-seat Atwood Cafe is popular with the pre- and post-theater crowds. That makes it perfect for the solo diner who might wish to feed after 8:00 P.M. Cuisine is traditional American with a twist: Comfy burgers and potpies nestle alongside more adventuresome offerings such as duck and manchego quesadillas. The formal tea with lavish desserts is also a treat if you're on your own and in the area. Service is smooth, but the Cafe can be quite noisy when busy or crowded.

Becco D'Oro

Radisson Hotel
160 East Huron
312-787-1300
$ $ $ $

More than you'd expect from a restaurant in a Radisson hotel, this Northern Italian newbie is nice—nice service, nice food, nice ambience. What it's not is exciting; if you're looking for eye-opening cuisine or inspiring decor, look elsewhere. That said, there's a pretty patio for warm-weather months, and solo diners (inside or outside) are treated respectfully. Tables are well-spaced and lighting is very comfortable. Menu leans toward the classics; wines are marked up considerably.

Bin 36
House of Blues Hotel
339 North Dearborn
312-755-WINE (9463)
$ $ $

Bin 36 is three options in one. The Market is a retail wine store; The Tavern serves wine and appetizers like steamed mussels, pizzas, and pâtés. And The Cellar offers full-service, contemporary American concoctions like diver-harvested sea scallops, farm-raised striped bass with kalamata mashed potatoes, and homemade butternut squash ravioli. While food and wine options typically get good reviews, service can be downright bad, and the music in the dining room can be very loud. Solo diners, take a tip: Enjoy a glass or flight of fine wine and a light bite in the more comfortable Tavern, a lounge space with comfortable seating next to the oval zinc bar, and bypass the dining room altogether. P.S. This place is right next door to the House of Blues, so you can enjoy some music after your meal.

Caliterra
Wyndham Chicago
633 North St. Clair
312-274-4444

$ $ $

Far from the madding Michigan Avenue crowd, Caliterra is one of Chicago's best-kept culinary secrets, with a menu of Italian/Californian fusion experiments that has tongues wagging and panting. For example, potato gnocchi is mated with lobster Bolognese or a bruschetta made from polenta, rosemary, and mascarpone. The space here is as clever as the cuisine, with a display kitchen to one side and a jazz lounge to the other, making Caliterra perfect for people-watching solo diners.

Cielo

Omni Chicago
676 North Michigan
312-944-7676
$ $ $

Noise-sensitive solo diners might want to stay away at happy hour, when the volume here gets cranked up several notches. But at any other time, the fabulous views of Michigan Avenue make this a perfect venue for solo diners to stare out the window and contemplate. Stiff competition for your attention from the solid Italianate menu, which some Chicagoans feel is highly underappreciated. Though this is a good medium-priced option, service is best described as decent.

Coq d'Or

The Drake Hotel
140 East Walton
312-787-2200
$ $ $

The Coq d'Or sort of disappears in the shade of the Cape Cod Room, the Drake's famous seafood restaurant. But this dark and cozy piano bar has had a full menu and amiable service for about as long as its better-known sibling. Because the Coq d'Or can be quite dark, it's best for people-watching solo diners rather than read-aholics. Drinks—which are great—are grain and cocktails rather than wine, whose offerings are limited. While the place looks like a men's-only club, women dining solo will find it comfortable and nonthreatening.

Grill on the Alley

Westin Hotel
909 North Michigan
312-255-9009
$ $ $

Another chain clone—this one a knockoff of a Beverly Hills legend—Grill on the Alley is a pleasant upscale steakhouse, but not more. Solo diners will find the decor (masculine, dark, wood/leather) and menu they'd expect, along with solicitous service and well-prepared, familiar food. A comfortable, if unremarkable, place for an unchallenging evening meal. P.S. The full dinner menu here is served until 1:00 A.M.

Iron Mike's Grille
Tremont Hotel
100 East Chestnut
312-587-8989

$ $ $

Call it Dikta's; call it Iron Mike's Grille; call it former Bears coach Mike Ditka's take on traditional Chicago steak and pasta cuisine and sports-team mania. You'll find banks of TVs; Ditka and other sports souvenirs for sale; and a menu where appetizers are called kick-offs and almost all offerings are priced to end with .20 (in case you don't know which Superbowl Ditka won). Solo diners will appreciate the comfortable barstools and booths with good views of the bar television. Curiously, the menu includes such boys club no-nos as duck wrapped in phyllo and seared tuna. The noise level is high, the lights are low, and the wines by the glass are limited. If you go, go for the scene. P.S. "Da Coach" stops by occasionally, but an imminent breakup with his partner was rumored at the time of this writing.

Park Avenue Cafe
The Doubletree Guest Suites
198 East Delaware Place
312-944-4414

$ $ $ $ ♯ ♯ ♯ ♯

♙ ♙ ♙   Ⴠ Ⴠ Ⴠ

♟ ♟ ♟   ⋒ ⋒ ⋒

The Park Avenue Cafe is the Windy City branch of the New York establishment, making it second helpings for the second city. The Solo Diner has issues with branded partnering and minichains, especially as Chicago has far too many branches of New York standards already (Le Colonial and others). But Park Avenue Cafe performs well. The swordfish chop here and the cured salmon live up to world-class standards, and the prix fixe brunch of American appetizers served dim sum style stands on its own. There is also a five-course tastings menu. Service is smooth; wines by the glass are better than average. Though some find the lighting low, it's more a place for reading than for writing or people watching.

The Dining Room

The Ritz Carlton
160 East Pearson
312-266-1000

$ $ $ $ ♯ ♯ ♯ ♯ ♯

♙ ♙ ♙ ♙ ♙   Ⴠ Ⴠ Ⴠ Ⴠ

♟ ♟ ♟   ⋒ ⋒ ⋒ ⋒

How good is the food here? So good that most diners don't notice—or don't care—that the service doesn't quite meet the standards set by the kitchen. Still, for solo diners looking to get pampered, this is the place; the room oozes luxury. The chef here is James Beard Foundation Award–winner Sarah Stegner, who is known for using infused oils and vegetable reductions to provide full flavor with only a fraction of the fat. Unlike many of its sibling Ritz Carltons, the Chicago Dining Room boasts a vegetarian degustation as well as more than twenty cheeses. Lighting is subdued, but good enough to read.

Seasons

Four Seasons Hotel
100 East Delaware Place
312-280-8800

$ $ $ $

This ultradeluxe property can feel intimidating when you step off the elevator into the sixth-floor lobby. So it's a pleasant surprise that Seasons, its highly regarded restaurant, carries the five-star amenities without the pretensions. Many local and visiting solo diners are Seasons regulars; the hotel attracts well-heeled business travelers, and Four Seasons condo owners breakfast or dine here frequently on their own. There's good reason; the room is bright, comfortable, and thoughtfully arranged (though acoustics permit eavesdropping from across the room). The food is forward thinking and clean. And the service strikes the perfect balance between friendly and unobtrusive. On a recent visit, a chilled golden tomato bisque was intense and bracing; a Japanese bento box entree with seared tuna, Chinese chicken salad, spring rolls, and grilled shrimp was both light and substantial; and homemade sorbets were lively and refreshing. If the Solo Diner could afford it, he'd become a regular here. P.S. Exquisite list of wines by the glass.

Shula's Steakhouse

Sheraton Chicago Hotel & Towers
301 East North Water
312-670-0788
$ $ $

Shula's is a fine place for a fine steak, but it's not really a Chicago kind of place. First, it's a gustatory shrine to Don Shula's career, with lots more pictures of Michael Jordan than there are of Chicago Bears. Second, no one from Chicago really eats here—but at least that means the staff will ask you where you're from and won't think it a bit odd that you're alone. Finally, any hard-core local fan with Midwestern values who ponies up $65.95 to attempt to chow down an entire forty-eight-ounce porterhouse is going to expect Shula's to throw in at least a tater for free. For that kind of money, you should be getting more than a few measly mushrooms on the side. With so much at stake, don't make an ordering decision until your server wheels up the cart of football-sized, plastic-wrapped slabs of prime, raw meat and proceeds to walk you through your carnivorous options. Listen carefully; the ovoid menus here are hard to read. P.S. No pigskin in the dining room, unless you count the menu printed on the Don Shula–autographed footballs ($295, available for carryout).

we

W Chicago City Center
172 West Adams
312-332-1200

$ $ $

⚁ ⚁ ⚁ ⚁

🍴 🍴 🍴 🍴

🍴 🍴 🍴 🍴

Y Y Y Y

�𝄢 ⲙ ⲙ ⲙ ⲙ

This hyperstylish downtown outpost of the fast-growing national W chain—once the dowdy Midland Hotel—works hard to create a happening scene in the lobby "Living Room" lounge and adjoining Whiskey Blue bar. So it's a pleasant surprise that we is not only surprisingly serious about food, but actually feels like a retreat from the hotel's hustle. Five small tables, perfect for solo diners, line the wall as you enter, and on quiet nights you can even request one of the plush purple banquettes opposite. One of the idiosyncratic elements here is a menu that lets you mix and match ingredients from three columns; the Solo Diner chose to go "straight across," the chef's choice, with wonderful results. Baby artichoke salad with arugula was beautifully presented; roasted halibut over sweet-and-sour cabbage was snow-white and perfectly cooked; and a dessert of warm banana turnovers was odd but delicious. Service is friendlier than you'd expect, and the Financial District location means they're accustomed to solo diners here on business. Very good lighting; serviceable list of wines by the glass. P.S. At press time, a sister property, W Lakeshore, was scheduled to open at 664 North Lake Shore Drive, near Navy Pier, with its own restaurants.

THE TABLE FOR ONE
HALL OF FAME

THERE ARE A number of places in Chicago that represent the best of everything solo diners would want at a table for one. Those establishments have been inducted into the Table for One Hall of Fame; long may they reign. In alphabetical order:

1. **Albert's Cafe**, 52 West Elm
   A cozy slice of Europe where you can hide yourself away.

2. **Ann Sather**, locations in Lakeview and on the North side
   Always a seat for one at this Swedish family table.

3. **Hilary's Urban Eatery**, 1500 West Division
   Still more counter than table seating.

4. **JT Collins**, 3358 North Paulina
   Neighborhood watering hole with above average pub grub where you'll feel like everyone knows your name.

5. **The Outpost**, 3438 North Clark
   Downtown quality dining with a neighborhood feel
   that solo diners will appreciate.

6. **Pasta Palazzo**, 1966 North Halsted
   Short-order Italian complete with counter seats.

7. **The Signature Room** on the Ninety-Fifth Floor of
   the John Hancock Building, 875 North Michigan
   Daydream by yourself in the best room with a view
   of the city made affordable and easy with an all-you-
   can-eat lunch buffet.

8. **Silver Cloud**, 1700 North Damen
   A comfy hideaway among all the Bucktown/Wicker
   Park hype.

9. **Villa Kula**, 4518 North Lincoln
   Teahouse and tea garden offering a serene, full high
   tea for one.

10. **Zoom Kitchen**, locations in The Loop, on Michigan
    Avenue, in Lakeview, and on the West side
    The freshest, fastest food for one.

The Table for One
Hall of Shame

FINALLY, WE'RE THRILLED to present the Table for One Hall of Shame—ten establishments that do their best to turn your solo dining experience into an extended episode of psychological warfare. We've suffered so you don't have to. Drum roll, please:

1. **Cheesecake Factory**, 875 North Michigan
   You'd have to be nuts to wait in this crazy zoo.

2. **Mia Francesca**, 3311 North Clark
   Always crowded and noisy, tight tables and, despite the reputation, mediocre food.

3. **Mirai Sushi**, 2020 West Division
   Too hip to have to welcome anyone warmly. Forget it without a reservation.

4. **mk**, 868 North Franklin
   Way too much attitude to cater to one, and trying to get your call answered for an all-important reservation is more hassle than you need.

5. **MOD**, 1520 North Damen
   Not unless you want to sit in the packed, smoky bar
   or be shoved into the communal table—and that's
   with a reservation.

6. **Nine**, 440 West Randolph (Wacker/Canal)
   You'd feel like an idiot sauntering down the staircase
   alone into the hipper-than-hip depths below.

7. **NoMi**, 800 North Michigan (Park Hyatt Hotel)
   Even single guests at the hotel shouldn't count on a
   warm welcome.

8. **Rambutan**, 2049 West Division
   No reservation, no way. Lots of attitude since
   moving to Wicker Park location.

9. **RL**, 115 East Chicago
   Full of poseurs suffering lousy service and lousy food
   while they check each other out.

10. **Zealous**, 419 West Superior
    The overly solicitous waitstaff in their matching
    flight attendant uniforms would make you crazy.

INDEX